Next Door SAVIOR

GUIDEBOOK

MAX LUCADO

W PUBLISHING GROUP™

www.wpublishinggroup.com

A Division of Thomas Nelson, Inc.
www.ThomasNelson.com

Published by W Publishing Group, a Division of Thomas Nelson, Inc., P.O. Box 141000, Nashville, Tennessee 37214.

All Scripture quotations, unless otherwise indicated, are taken from the *NEW AMERICAN STANDARD BIBLE®*, Copyright © 1960, 1962, 1963, 1968, 1971, 1972, 1973, 1975, 1977, 1995 by The Lockman Foundation. Used by permission.

Other Scripture references are from the following sources:

The *HOLY BIBLE, NEW INTERNATIONAL VERSION®*. Copyright © 1973, 1978, 1984 by International Bible Society. Used by permission of Zondervan Publishing House. All rights reserved. The "NIV" and "New International Version" trademarks are registered in the United States Patent and Trademark Office by International Bible Society. Use of either trademark requires the permission of International Bible Society.

The Living Bible copyright © 1971 (TLB). Used by permission of Tyndale House Publishers, Inc., Wheaton, Illinois 60189. All rights reserved.

The *Holy Bible,* New Living Translation (NLT), copyright © 1996. Used by permission of Tyndale House Publishers, Inc., Wheaton, Illinois 60189. All rights reserved.

THE AMPLIFIED BIBLE (AMP), copyright © 1954, 1958, 1962, 1964, 1965, 1987 by The Lockman Foundation. All rights reserved. Used by permission. (www.Lockman.org).

New Revised Standard Version Bible (NRSV), copyright 1989, Division of Christian Education of the National Council of the Churches of Christ in the United States of America.

The *New King James Version* (NKJV), copyright © 1979, 1980, 1982 by Thomas Nelson, Inc. Used by permission. All rights reserved.

THE MESSAGE (MSG), copyright © 1993, 1994, 1995, 1996, 2000, 2001, 2002. Used by permission of NavPress Publishing Group.

The Holy Bible, New Century Version (NCV), copyright © 1987, 1988, 1991 by Word Publishing, Dallas, Texas 75234. Used by permission.

The *Contemporary English Version* (CEV), copyright © 1995, American Bible Society. Used by permission. All rights reserved.

The *Today's English Version* Bible (TEV), copyright © 1976, 1992, American Bible Society. Used by permission. All rights reserved.

Quoted material used in this book is taken from *Next Door Savior,* © 2003 by Max Lucado, published by W Publishing Group.

Other quotations taken from: *No Wonder They Call Him the Savior, God Came Near, And the Angels Were Silent,* and *Six Hours One Friday*

Produced with the assistance of The Livingstone Corporation (www.LivingstoneCorp.com). Project staff includes Dave Veerman and Mary Horner Collins.

ISBN 0-8499-4480-5

Printed in the United States of America
04 05 06 07 VG 9 8 7 6 5 4 3 2 1

Table of Contents

Introduction

"Why a Next Door Savior Guidebook?"

Perhaps that's your thought as you pick up this book. Maybe a friend or family member gave it to you. Or you're standing in a bookstore skimming these pages. It's a fair question. And the answer is simple. "Some books are to be tasted," Francis Bacon wisely observed, "others are to be swallowed, and some are to be chewed and digested." Max Lucado's *Next Door Savior* fits that third category. It's an important book if only because it focuses on the most important, most amazing person the world has ever known.

This guidebook is designed to help you "chew and digest" the truth about Jesus. It has been created with the hope that you will encounter Christ in new ways—and that you will meditate on his words and works until they sink deeply into your heart and soul and become central to how you think, how you see the world, and, most importantly, how you live.

"HOW DO I USE THIS RESOURCE?"

Each chapter in this *Next Door Savior Guidebook* corresponds to a chapter in the *Next Door Savior* book. Each lesson contains six components:

- **Impressions:** This section gives you the opportunity to jot down your initial gut reaction to the content of the corresponding chapter in the book. By verbalizing your questions, emotions, doubts, uncertainties, and so forth, you will begin the process of gaining insight into who Christ is, what you think of him, and perhaps how your thinking needs to change.

- **Glimpses:** On most occasions this section takes you straight into the Bible for a first-hand look at Jesus (conversations he had, miracles he performed, places and people he visited). Other times the **Glimpses** will direct you to passages written *about* Jesus by those who knew him or were associates of his closest followers. These **Glimpses** are, in a real sense, written snapshots. They give you an up close and personal peek into the next door Savior's life. A number of different Bible translations will be used in this guidebook, and most of these passages will be provided for you.

- **Musings:** This section asks a number of thought-provoking questions about Jesus. The goal here is to ponder the personal and eternal implications of Jesus' life and claims. Let these musings spark your curiosity, foster deeper understanding, and stimulate a true sense of wonder. Hopefully, your mind will be spinning—in a good sense—as you contemplate the amazing "next door Savior."

- **Encounters:** These contain a simple quote by Max Lucado and nothing else—just lots of space for you to journal. The only limits here are your imagination. You may choose to write out a confession, describe the deepest cry of your heart, or compose a poem or song of praise. List any questions you have. Or your needs. Your secret dreams. Your deepest hopes. Go ahead. It really *is* okay to struggle and wrestle with the truth. Jot it all down. Try to describe what God is teaching you or, better, how Christ is *touching* you through your study. In years to come, this record of spiritual encounter will become one of your most treasured possessions.

- **Decisions:** Someone has noted that the goal of the Christian faith isn't information, it's transformation. God didn't give us his Word to make us smarter sinners; he gave us his Truth to make us holier saints. With that wise counsel in mind, this section seeks to help you apply the Bible to life. You will ask, in so many words, "So what?" That is, "How does this, how *should* this alter the way I think and talk and live?"

- **Reminders:** This is simply a concise, easy-to-remember summary of each chapter.

"ANY FINAL ADVICE?"

As you begin this journey, a little common sense counsel is in order.

Pray. Before you sit down to wrestle with these lessons, solicit God's help, his wisdom, and insight. Ask him to open the eyes of your heart (Ephesians 1:18). Ask him to make you receptive to whatever he wants to show you, to however he wants to change you. Ask Jesus to meet you in a real way. And make sure you request protection and the ability to persevere. Why? Our enemy, the devil, *hates* the thought of your developing a closer walk with Christ. When he discovers what you're doing, be assured that he will try everything he can to divert you and discourage you.

Take your time. There's no need to rush. This isn't a race. You don't get an award for finishing first. The prize you *will* get, if you are thoughtful and deliberate, is a deeper, more meaningful relationship with Jesus.

Read. Take *Next Door Savior* a chapter at a time. Begin by reading chapter 1 of the book, underlining or highlighting sentences or phrases that stand out to you. Then go to the guidebook and work through the corresponding lesson.

Think. In this impatient and distracted age, pondering deeply is a lost art. About the only people who meditate anymore are Eastern mystics. What a shame! Meditation is simply mulling something over in one's mind, considering it from every possible angle. *Biblical* meditation is letting God's truth permeate our being. We consider it and think on it, deliberately allowing it to sink from our heads deeply into our hearts, so that it ultimately shapes the way we live. Don't forget, the Bible tells us to love God with all our hearts and *minds* (see Matthew 22:37). In another place, God pleads, "Come now and let us *reason* together" (Isaiah 1:18, emphasis added). The point? Time spent lost in thought about Christ isn't wasted, it's *commanded!* And, in fact, it is crucial to a richer spiritual life.

Listen. The Bible is called God's written Word, and Jesus is known as the living Word of God (John 1:14). Why the fuss about "words"? Because God is speaking. He longs for you to hear his voice, so that you might know his love for you and embrace his gracious and good plans for your life. Whatever else you do as you work through these pages, please make sure you have, in the words of Christ, "ears to hear."

Be honest. Don't give in to the pressure to fill your guidebook with nice-sounding Sunday school answers. Perhaps it's because we worry that someone will find our notebook someday that we succumb to the temptation to put a positive spin on our responses. We answer creatively, to make ourselves look more noble, to make it appear as though we have it together. Don't do that. Instead, be honest and write from your heart. Remember, the truth is what sets us free.

Invite someone to join you. Perhaps your spouse, a neighbor, a friend, or a colleague—anyone who can make the journey with you. When the process gets hard (and it will), you'll have each other to lean on. You will have a spiritual companion who can spur you on when you feel like quitting. You may even wish to form a small group and work through these lessons together. That's entirely up to you.

Remember the goal. Use this guidebook to come face-to-face and heart-to-heart with Jesus Christ. Think of each session as a visit on the front porch or a friendly conversation over the back fence . . . with your next door Savior.

"May the God of peace, who through the blood of the eternal covenant brought back from the dead our Lord Jesus, that great Shepherd of the sheep, equip you with everything good for doing his will, and may he work in us what is pleasing to him, through Jesus Christ, to whom be glory for ever and ever. Amen." (Hebrews 13:20–21 NIV)

"Near enough to touch. Strong enough to trust. A next door Savior."

1

Our Next Door Savior

"Something is absurd. . . . God doesn't chum with the common folk or snooze in fishing boats. But according to the Bible he did. 'For in Christ there is all of God in a human body' (Colossians 2:9 TLB). Jesus was not a godlike man, nor a manlike God. He was God-man." (pp. 4–5)

IMPRESSIONS

What was your first reaction to chapter one of *Next Door Savior*? How did it affect you? What emotions and questions did it stir in you? What passages or thoughts jumped out?

What is your mental picture of Jesus? Where do you think you got this notion of Christ?

Of the "Jesus" films you have seen, which is your favorite? Which one did you like the least? Overall, what is your impression of these assorted cinematic biographies of Christ?

As you begin, pray that "the eyes of your heart may be enlightened" (Ephesians 1:18) during this time of reflection and study.

GLIMPSES

Matthew 16:13–16
Now when Jesus came into the district of Caesarea Philippi, He was asking His disciples, "Who do people say that the Son of Man is?" And they said, "Some say John the Baptist; and others, Elijah;

but still others, Jeremiah, or one of the prophets." He said to them, "But who do you say that I am?" Simon Peter answered, "You are the Christ, the Son of the living God."

Put yourself in this scene. Better yet, update the scene. Change it a bit. Imagine you're at a dinner party, and the guests begin discussing the latest issue of a popular news magazine—the one that contains a controversial cover story about Jesus.

What comments or descriptions would you hear about Christ? What would *you* say?

Which is easier and why—to report what other people are saying about Jesus or to figure out what *you* personally believe? Why?

What do the following passages reveal about Jesus?
Colossians 2:9

Philippians 3:8–11

It's no secret that the disciples (until *after* Christ rose from the dead) were a flaky, shaky bunch. Devoted one day, they doubted the next. In the instance above, Peter got the right answer. Yet in the days and weeks to come, he would make plenty of wrong choices.

Why is putting our faith in Christ so difficult? Why is living by faith even harder?

Encounters

"The cache of Christianity is Christ." (p. 6)

How does it make you feel to realize that even the so-called "giants of the faith" (for example, men like the apostle Peter) struggled to come to terms with the identity of Jesus?

MUSINGS

Who is Jesus? Don't answer in the way you think you're *supposed* to answer—respond according to what's really in your heart and mind. What do you honestly think about the carpenter from Nazareth? Was he a good man, a prophet, a victim of circumstances, a faith-healer, a wise teacher, or what?

Circle the titles or descriptions of Jesus that mean the most to you right now in your stage of life.

Savior	Lamb of God
Lord or Lord of lords	Good Shepherd
Christ/Messiah	Holy One of God
Friend of sinners	Son of man
King or King of kings	Healer
Judge	Redeemer
Rabbi	

> "All the splendor of heaven revealed in a human body. For a period ever so brief, the doors to the throne room were open and God came near. His Majesty was seen. Heaven touched the earth and, as a result, earth can know heaven."
>
> —GOD CAME NEAR

Why did you choose those?

God Came Near

On a spiritual satisfaction scale of 1 to 10 (1 = empty and 10 = ultimate fulfillment), what is the current state of your soul?

What would you like to say to Jesus right now?

Encounters

"As we behold him, we become like him." (p. 6)

DECISIONS

"My idea is simple. Let's look at some of the places he went and some people he touched. Join me on a quest for his 'Godmanness.' You may be amazed." (p. 6)

What do you think Max means by the term "Godmanness"?

What are the implications if Jesus really is who he claims to be?

What *concerns* do you have as you begin this experiment?

What *questions* do you have as you begin this adventure?

> "God did what we wouldn't dare dream. He did what we couldn't imagine. He became a man so we could trust him. He became a sacrifice so we could know him. And he defeated death, so we could follow him."
>
> —AND THE ANGELS WERE SILENT

Is there a friend you would like to invite to join you?

REMINDERS

- Jesus, the Nazarene carpenter who lived 2,000 years ago, claimed to be God in the flesh.
- Jesus' life (his flawless character and undeniable miracles) backs up his astounding claims.
- Nothing is more important than getting to know Jesus.
- We are changed forever when we encounter Jesus.

2
Christ's Theme Song

Every Person

> *"Jesus displays the bad apples of his family tree in the first chapter of the New Testament. You've barely dipped a toe into Matthew's gospel when you realize Jesus hails from the Tilted Halo Society. Rahab was a Jericho harlot. Grandpa Jacob was slippery enough to warrant an electric ankle bracelet. David had a personality as irregular as a Picasso painting—one day writing psalms, another day seducing his captain's wife. But did Jesus erase his name from the list? Not at all." (p. 13)*

IMPRESSIONS

Chapter 2 of *Next Door Savior* isn't very long, but it's packed with verbal pictures and thought-provoking facts about Jesus. How did you feel as you were reading? What surprised you? Startled you? Amused you?

Why do you think the Lord made his entrance into the world in such a non-descript way, in such a nowhere place, and under such eyebrow-raising circumstances?

If you were writing the story of the universe and were devising a way to rescue a doomed creation, how might your version be different than God's?

As you begin this time of reflection, pray that you will have "ears to hear" whatever Jesus is trying to say to you.

GLIMPSES

Hebrews 2:17–18 (MSG)

He had to enter into every detail of human life. Then, when he came before God as high priest to get rid of the people's sins, he would have already experienced it all himself—all the pain, all the testing—and would be able to help where help was needed.

"Every detail of human life," . . . except sin. How did Christ manage to enter our world and experience human existence fully—yet without sinning? Why was it necessary that Jesus *not* sin?

Max cites all kinds of situations, emotions, and trials that Jesus faced. Which of the following connection points do you share with Christ? (Check all that apply.)

_____ A family tree with some bad apples or questionable characters

_____ Loneliness

_____ Discouragement

_____ Being from a nowhere hometown

_____ Raised by a single parent

_____ From a lower-income family

_____ Average looks

_____ Dealing with stressful leadership pressures

_____ People making constant demands on you

_____ A victim of false accusations

_____ Misunderstood by family and friends

_____ Hated and mistreated by the powerful

_____ Abandoned by friends

Right now, what is your greatest trial or source of stress? Why? Based on what you've read and studied so far, what do you think Jesus might be saying to you?

Encounters

"He may look like as common as the guy next door, but just wait. . . ." (p. 6)

What do the following Bible passages reveal about Jesus?
Luke 2:22–24

Mark 6:3

Isaiah 53:2

Mark 1:35

Mark 6:31

Mark 3:21

> A young man, a plumber by trade, in your town starts claiming to be God in the flesh. You do a little checking and discover he was born behind the dumpsters at the Motel 6 some eighty miles down the road, to an unwed mother. What would you think?

MUSINGS

"Jesus had . . . common looks. 'No stately form or majesty that we should look upon Him, nor appearance that we should be attracted to Him' (Isaiah 53:2). Drop dead smile? Steal-your-breath physique? No. Heads didn't turn when Jesus passed. If he was anything like his peers, he had a broad peasant's face, dark olive skin, short curly hair, and a prominent nose. He stood five feet one inch tall and weighed around 110 pounds. Hardly worth a GQ cover. According to a third-century historian, Origen, "his body was small and ill-shapen and ignoble." (p. 14)

Is this a new thought to you? How is it different from how you've imagined Jesus looking?

If this description is true, if Jesus of Nazareth really *wasn't* "much to look at," how could he have been so popular with the masses?

Encounters

"You never outgrow the urge to look up and say, 'Help!'" (p. 10)

"Jesus has been there. He experienced 'all the pain, all the testing' (Hebrews 2:18 MSG). Jesus was angry enough to purge the temple, hungry enough to eat raw grain, distraught enough to weep in public, fun loving enough to be called a drunkard, winsome enough to attract kids, weary enough to sleep in a storm-bounced boat, poor enough to sleep on dirt and borrow a coin for a sermon illustration, radical enough to get kicked out of town, responsible enough to care for his mother, tempted enough to know the smell of Satan, and fearful enough to sweat blood. But why? Why would heaven's finest Son endure earth's toughest pain? So you would know that 'he is able . . . to run to the cry of . . . those who are being tempted and tested and tried' (Hebrews 2:18 AMP)." (p. 16)

When you are tired, discouraged, guilty, sad, angry, or _____ (name the emotion), do you *really*—in your heart of hearts—believe that Christ knows exactly how you feel and that he cares? Why or why not?

What words best describe your reaction to the news that, humanly speaking, Jesus descended from a long line of questionable characters?

DECISIONS

"He's not ashamed of you. Nor is he confused by you. Your actions don't bewilder him. Your tilted halo doesn't trouble him. So go to him. After all, you're part of his family." (p. 17)

According to John 1:12, how exactly does a person become part of God's family?

Encounters

"An ordinary laborer with ordinary looks. Can you spot him?" (p. 14)

Have you ever received Christ—that is, put your trust in him, acknowledged Jesus as the only one who can make you right with God and give you eternal life? If so, describe that experience and how it has changed your life.

If you have never done so, would you like to embrace Christ as your Next Door Savior right now? Write out a simple prayer that expresses your desire to know Christ and to follow him.

Write down the names of three people you intend to tell about your newfound devotion to Christ.

REMINDERS

- Jesus Christ is fully divine.
- In taking on full humanity (becoming a man), Christ experienced every human emotion, temptation, and pressure.
- Because Jesus lived on earth among his creatures for thirty-three plus years, he fully understands what you are up against. He has been there.
- Jesus is not ashamed of you (Hebrews 2:11); in fact, he is *wildly in love* with you (Romans 8:35–39)!

3
Friend of Flops

Shady People

"Quite a story. Matthew goes from double-dealer to disciple. He throws a party that makes the religious right uptight, but Christ proud. . . . Some story indeed." (p. 24)

IMPRESSIONS

What do you remember most vividly about chapter 3 of *Next Door Savior?* If it's been a few days since you read it, take five minutes and skim back over the content. What jumps out at you? What questions do you have? Where does the chapter cause you to go in your own heart and mind?

Using weather terminology, how would you describe your life right now?
_____ Cold! Frigid! An artic blast right through the heart!
_____ Balmy and breezy
_____ Scorching hot!
_____ Cloudy with a 70 percent chance of drizzling rain
_____ Thunderstorms with possible flash flooding
_____ Tornado warning!
_____ Other:

Explain in more detail the "how" and "why" of your "personal forecast."

Imagine Jesus paying a "physical visit" to your city or town—suddenly he just shows up in the flesh. Where do you think he might hang out? What sort of people might he seek out?

As you begin this time of deeper reflection, pray that you might deeply experience the unconditional grace and acceptance of the one called "the friend of sinners."

GLIMPSES

Matthew 9:9–13 (NLT) gives us a peek into this scene:

> As Jesus was going down the road, he saw Matthew sitting at his tax-collection booth. "Come, be my disciple," Jesus said to him. So Matthew got up and followed him. That night Matthew invited Jesus and his disciples to be his dinner guests, along with his fellow tax collectors and many other notorious sinners. The Pharisees were indignant. "Why does your teacher eat with such scum?" they asked his disciples.
>
> When he heard this, Jesus replied, "Healthy people don't need a doctor—sick people do." Then he added, "Now go and learn the meaning of this Scripture: 'I want you to be merciful; I don't want your sacrifices.' For I have come to call sinners, not those who think they are already good enough."

Tax collectors like Matthew (or Levi, according to his given name) were despised, loathed, hated, abhorred, detested . . . (starting to get the picture?) by their Jewish countrymen. What occupations in our culture and era might similarly be frowned upon?

Put yourself in Matthew's place. You are going about your day, your life, and suddenly this provocative and popular rabbi is calling you to follow him. What would motivate you to do so? What must have been happening inside Matthew?

What did the Pharisees and religious highbrows of his day think of Jesus' choice of friends and disciples?

Read Luke 19:1–10. In what ways is this story of Zaccheus similar to the story of the call of Matthew?

Encounters

"*Whatever you are facing, he knows how you feel.*" (p. 16)

What does it say to you that Jesus went out of his way to pick a shady character like Matthew to be one of his most intimate followers?

MUSINGS

Do you think Jesus was funny and fun to be around? Can you picture Christ laughing and joking with his disciples? With Matthew's irreligious buddies? Why or why not?

When the "religious police" crashed Matthew's party and began turning up their noses at all the irreligious people in attendance, Jesus said, "Healthy people don't need a doctor—sick people do." What do you think he meant? Was he putting down Matthew and his friends?

Augustine noted, "You have made us for Yourself, O God, and our hearts are restless until they find rest in You." Mark Twain was reported to have sighed, "You don't know quite what it is that you want, but it just fairly makes your heart ache, you want it so." In what ways is this kind of desperation, emptiness, and restlessness *good*?

How restless are *you* just now?

DECISIONS

"You and I are Matthew. Don't look at me that way. There's enough hustler in the best of us to qualify for Matthew's table. Maybe you've never taken taxes, but you've taken liberty with the truth, taken credit that wasn't yours, taken advantage of the weak. You and me? Matthew." (p. 24)
When we read the Gospels, we are struck by the

"What are you doing with God's personal request that you live with him forever? That is the only decision that really matters. Whether or not you take the job transfer is not crucial. What college you choose or what profession you select is important, but not compared to where you spend eternity. That is the decision you will remember. What are you doing with his invitation?

—AND THE ANGELS WERE SILENT

Encounters

_____

_____

_____

_____

_____

_____

_____

_____

_____

_____

_____

_____

_____

_____

_____

"When you turn to him for help, he runs to you to help." (p. 16)

fact that sinful, messed-up people were attracted to Jesus. They sought him out! And yet, today most irreligious folks avoid church and Christians like the plague. Why do you think? What has happened?

> "God is the shepherd in search of his lamb. His legs are scratched, his feet are sore and his eyes are burning. He scales the cliffs and traverses the fields. He explores the caves. He cups his hands to his mouth and calls into the canyon. And the name he calls is yours."
>
> —AND THE ANGELS WERE SILENT

Next Door Savior lists all the surprising kinds of people whom Jesus sought out. Which of the following best describe you at this point in life? (You may check more than one).

_____ Shady   _____ Tormented

_____ Desperate   _____ Spiritually weary

_____ Discouraged   _____ Imperfect

_____ Suffering   _____ Other:

_____ Grieving

When have you felt—really experienced—the unconditional love and acceptance of Christ? When have you heard him call your name, beckoning you to follow him? What did you do? What happened?

What current or old friends of yours need to meet the Next Door Savior, the friend of flops? Matthew threw a party. What everyday hobby or event can *you* use to introduce your friends to Jesus?

If you're just finding out about Christ and haven't yet decided to become his friend and follower, how does this story alter your view of him? What's keeping you from responding to his invitation?

Encounters

"You don't have to be weird to follow Jesus." (p. 24)

REMINDERS

- Jesus came to seek and befriend and change—forever!—shady people.
- Guess what? We're *all* shady people. We're all flops—quirky, insecure creatures with lots of failure in our rearview mirror.
- Christ not only wants to forgive you, but also to use you to reach those in your circle of influence with the amazing news that they, too, are loved and accepted, no strings attached!

4
The Hand God Loves to Hold

Desperate People

"Jesus can heal. And Jesus is coming." (p. 30)

IMPRESSIONS

If you're having difficulty connecting with God in these sessions, do something different. Shake things up. Why? Well, remember the old saying, "If you keep doing what you've been doing, you'll keep getting what you've been getting!" It's wise counsel. The idea is that a little change can sometimes jolt us out of a rut. So, weather permitting, change your scenery. Read chapter 4 of *Next Door Savior* and work through this chapter of your guidebook in a park, at the beach, by a stream, or on your patio. Go to a place of quiet beauty. Take a few minutes before you begin and listen to (or sing) a few praise choruses.

Most importantly, get still—absolutely still—and let God begin to speak to your heart. Listen carefully. He wants you to know him. He wants you to hear him. He's got a message just for you.

First, a little personal reflection: How would you best describe your relationship with Jesus Christ right now?

_____ Skeptical seeker (you're not sure *what* to think!)

_____ Curious disciple (a learner hungry to know more)

_____ Devoted follower

_____ Other: _____

Add some detail to that description.

In the hit movie *City Slickers* one of the main characters asks his buddies a good two-part question: "What was the *best* day of your life, and what was the *worst* day of your life?" How would you answer? (Use one of the "Encounters" journal pages if you need more space.)

When have you felt the most desperate? What caused this state of hopelessness? What did you end up doing?

As you begin working through this chapter in the *Next Door Savior Guidebook*, ask the Lord for wisdom, discernment, and insight. Mostly, ask him to come close enough to touch.

Glimpses

Mark 5:25–34 (NLT)

And there was a woman in the crowd who had had a hemorrhage for twelve years. She had suffered a great deal from many doctors through the years and had spent everything she had to pay them, but she had gotten no better. In fact, she was worse. She had heard about Jesus, so she came up behind him through the crowd and touched the fringe of his robe. For she thought to herself, "If I can just touch his clothing, I will be healed." Immediately the bleeding stopped, and she could feel that she had been healed!

Jesus realized at once that healing power had gone out from him, so he turned around in the crowd and asked, "Who touched my clothes?"

His disciples said to him, "All this crowd is pressing around you. How can you ask, 'Who touched me?'" But he kept on looking around to see who had done it. Then the frightened woman, trembling at the realization of what had happened to her, came and fell at his feet and told him what she had done.

And he said to her, "Daughter, your faith has made you well. Go in peace. You have been healed."

Imagine this woman's twelve-year fight to get relief from a worsening medical condition. Twelve years! Think back over that many years in your own life. That's a long time, isn't it? Try to put some words and descriptive phrases to what this woman's experience must have been like.

Encounters

_____

_____

_____

_____

_____

_____

_____

_____

_____

_____

_____

_____

_____

_____

_____

_____

_____

_____

"Following me doesn't mean forgetting your friends. Just the opposite.
I want to meet them." (p. 23)

How would her life have turned out differently if, say, the first or second doctor she had consulted (back in year one) had been able to get her condition "under control"? What does this suggest to you?

Look at the words Jesus used in responding to the woman: "made you well," "go in peace," "you have been healed." How do these sentiments fit with the mission that Jesus announced for himself in Luke 4:14–19?

Realize the story of the bleeding woman represents a parenthesis within another story (see Mark 5: 21–43). A panicky, prominent synagogue official had convinced Jesus to come quickly and save his dying daughter. The man's entourage, on a time-sensitive life-and-death mission, was then interrupted by this anonymous bleeding woman.

Imagine being the official with a dying daughter back home. How do you feel as Jesus stops to locate and help this lowly woman in the midst of a massive crowd?

What does this incident show you about the power of Jesus? About his care for *every* individual?

MUSINGS

If you were granted the opportunity to go back in time and witness any of Jesus' miracles up close, which one would you choose and why?

By any standards, Jesus lived a full, often jam-packed life. And yet he never seemed stressed or hurried or frantic. Why do you think this was true? What was his secret? (Hint: See Mark 1:35 and John 8:29.)

> "Do you believe that God is near? He wants you to. He wants you to know that he is in the midst of your world. Wherever you are as you read these words, he is present. In your car. On the plane. In your office, your bedroom, your den. He's near. And he is more than near. He is active."
>
> —AND THE ANGELS WERE SILENT

Encounters

"You think I came to quarantine you?" (p. 23)

What situations, circumstances, and relationships in life bug you the most? Which ones really *haunt* you?

What is *the* most desperate situation in your life right now—the one that keeps you up at night and that you absolutely cannot fix? How does the biblical record of Christ healing the bleeding woman encourage you today?

> "You have two choices. You can reject Jesus. That is an option. You can, as have many, decide that the idea of God becoming a carpenter is too bizarre—and walk away. Or you can accept him. You can journey with him. You can listen for his voice amidst the hundreds of voices and follow him."
>
> —AND THE ANGELS WERE SILENT

DECISIONS

"Illness took her strength. What took yours? Red ink? Hard drink? Late nights in the wrong arms? Long days on the wrong job? Pregnant too soon? Too often? Is her hand your hand? If so, take heart. Your family may shun it. Society may avoid it. But Christ? Christ wants to touch it. When your hand reaches through the masses, he knows." (p. 31)

Why do so many Christians remain so blasé and unmoved when they read the Gospels? How do we avoid the trap of becoming numb to the amazing words and extraordinary works of Jesus?

Some people have a tendency to put Bible characters (even minor ones) in a special category, to view them as different, their situations as unique in history, and their stories as "interesting, but irrelevant." That's an erroneous view. God wanted these snapshots of real life preserved in his Word to give us an accurate picture of actual people who had undeniable encounters with heaven. His intent? To show us the kind of God he is, and to birth in us the faith that what he did *then*, he can do *now*.

What do you need from God—really *need*—right now? What is the deepest hunger of your heart?

Encounters

"Discipleship is sometimes defined by being normal." (p. 25)

This event from the life of Christ shows a next door Savior who is sensitive, searching, patient, and full of compassion. Is this *your* picture of Jesus? Why or why not?

When Christ left the earth, he commissioned his followers (the Church) to be his body. We are, according to the New Testament, his hands and mouth and feet in the world. So ponder for a moment: What people in your sphere of influence are feeling desperate and need to experience the loving touch of Christ? How specifically can *you* reach out to them this week?

REMINDERS

- Trial and tragedy do not discriminate. We *all* are eventually afflicted.
- Jesus offers help and hope to the desperate.
- He is always close by and never too busy for you.
- Reach out for Christ, and let him touch and heal your sorrow and pain.

5
Try Again

Discouraged People

"Is it too late for you? Before you say yes, before you fold up the nets and head for the house—two questions. Have you given Christ your boat? Your heartache? Your dead-end dilemma? Your struggle? Have you really turned it over to him?" (p. 39)

IMPRESSIONS

If you haven't already done so, take a few minutes to read chapter 5 of *Next Door Savior*, underlining or highlighting sentences or phrases that stand out to you.

What impresses you? Encourages you? Makes you smile?

If you go to Springfield, Illinois, and visit the historic Lincoln Home, you can stand in the very same hallowed parlor where the Great Emancipator himself once sat and conversed. It's an odd, exhilarating feeling. In the same way, if you go to modern-day Israel you can actually visit sites where *God* once walked and talked—in the person of Jesus Christ. Does that boggle your mind?

How does the truth of the "next door Savior" make you feel?

Think of your religious experiences in life. What have been the high points? The low points?

As you begin this time of reflection and study, pray the prayer of ancient King Jehoshaphat (2 Chronicles 20:12). He was confused and anxious, surrounded by a powerful enemy, and in need of divine direction. What did he do? He lifted his voice to heaven and cried: "O our God, . . . we are powerless. . . . We do not know what to do, but we are looking to you for help" (NLT). God loves it when his children cling desperately to him, in absolute dependence!

GLIMPSES

Chapter 5 of *Next Door Savior* focuses our attention on the events of Luke 5:1–11. Here's what happened:

> Now it happened that while the crowd was pressing around Him and listening to the word of God, He was standing by the lake of Gennesaret; and He saw two boats lying at the edge of the lake; but the fishermen had gotten out of them and were washing their nets. And He got into one of the boats, which was Simon's, and asked him to put out a little way from the land. And He sat down and began teaching the people from the boat. When He had finished speaking, He said to Simon, "Put out into the deep water and let down your nets for a catch." Simon answered and said, "Master, we worked hard all night and caught nothing, but do as I say and I will let down the nets." And when they had done this, they enclosed a great quantity of fish; and their nets began to break; they signaled to their partners in the other boat for them to come and help them. And they came and filled both of the boats, so that they began to sink. But when Simon Peter saw that, he fell down at Jesus' feet, saying, "Go away from me Lord, for I am a sinful man!" For amazement had seized him and all his companions because of the catch of fish which they had taken; and so also were James and John, sons of Zebedee, who were partners with Simon. And Jesus said to Simon, "Do not fear, from now on you will be catching men." When they had brought their boats to land, they left everything and followed Him.

Max writes: "Whatever thoughts Peter had were distilled to one phrase: 'We worked hard all night and caught nothing' (v. 5)." How do you think Peter (the exhausted professional fisherman) felt when Jesus, a carpenter-turned-rabbi, started giving him fishing instructions? Circle any and all words that describe his likely attitudes and tone:

Frustrated	Irritated	Optimistic	Annoyed	Tired
Cynical	Put out	Weary	Polite	Respectful
Condescending	Full of faith	Eager	Angry	Sarcastic

Encounters

"Her desperation births an idea." (p. 30)

What did this one incident cause Peter to realize about Jesus? How did it alter his life?

For Peter, this was the catch of a lifetime, yet he turned his back on the enormous pile of flopping fish. Why? What do you suppose happened in his heart?

What did Jesus mean when he said, "From now on, you will be catching men"?

> "Do you have any worn, wet, empty nets? Do you know the feeling of a sleepless, fishless night? Of course you do. For what have you been casting? Sobriety? 'I've worked so hard to stay sober, but . . .' Solvency? 'My debt is an anvil around my neck . . .' Faith? 'I want to believe, but . . .' Healing? 'I've been sick so long . . .' A happy marriage? 'No matter what I do . . .' I've worked hard all night and caught nothing."
>
> —NEXT DOOR SAVIOR

MUSINGS

What are your biggest questions in life? Or put it this way: If you could go to lunch tomorrow with Christ at your favorite restaurant, sit across the table from him, look him squarely in the eyes, ask him *anything*, and hear his audible response, what would you choose to talk about and why?

Luke 5:1–11 paints a picture of a fisherman who is utterly deflated by his empty nets. What empty places do you see in your life? Survey your situation. What discouraging circumstances prompt you to say, "Oh, that? That's just the way it is. It's too late to fix that or change that. *That* will never change!"?

Encounters

"Word among the lepers and the left out is this: Jesus can heal." (p. 30)

What is the most surprising, unexpected blessing God has ever dropped in your life?

What is the most surprising way God has used *you* to bring blessing to another's life?

Look hard at your life—your background, talents, personality, experiences, relationships, possessions, positions, opportunities, etc. How might God want to use all these gifts in your life for his glory and your ultimate fulfillment?

"Contrary to what you may have been told, Jesus doesn't limit his recruiting to the stout-hearted. The beat up and worn out are prime prospects in his book, and he's been known to climb into boats, bars, and brothels to tell them, 'It's not too late to start over.'"

—NEXT DOOR SAVIOR

DECISIONS

"And have you gone deep? Have you by-passed the surface-water solutions you can see in search of the deep-channel provisions God can give? Try the other side of the boat. Go deeper than you've gone. You may find what Peter found. The pay-load of his second effort was not the fish he caught but the God he saw." (p. 39–40)

Narrow your thinking to one circumstance in your life that you wish Jesus would change. You probably don't have to think too hard. What if it never changes? What if, for some reason known only to heaven, you have to live with this situation for the rest of your life—how will that affect your faith?

Encounters

"The woman feels power enter. . . . Jesus feels power exit." (p. 30)

What is the secret of perseverance? How do we continue to hang in there when we get that sinking feeling that things "will never change" and when everything within us wants to throw in the towel?

"I believe God has a graciously terrible memory. . . . If he didn't forget, how could we pray? How could we dare enter into his presence if the moment he saw us he remembered all our pitiful past? How could we enter his throne room wearing the rags of our selfishness and gluttony? We couldn't. And we don't. . . . We have "put on" Christ. When God looks at us, he doesn't see us; he sees Christ."

—GOD CAME NEAR

The Swiss psychiatrist and Christian author Paul Tournier once observed: "There are two things we cannot do alone. One is be married. The other is be a Christian." How can fellow believers in Jesus make a huge difference in your life as you struggle with your own "empty nets"? What does their involvement in your life look like this week? List the names of some Christian friends you can and will call upon this week.

It's been reported that Thomas Edison, in his quest to invent a reliable light bulb, failed more than a *thousand* times. Imagine if he had quit after his 657th unsuccessful attempt—perhaps you would be reading this sentence by candlelight! The point is, we *can't* quit. We can't let our empty nets defeat us. We have to be willing to follow Christ one more step, one more day, no matter what happened yesterday.

End your time of study and reflection by meditating on Galatians 6:9: "So don't get tired of doing what is good. Don't get discouraged and give up, for we will reap a harvest of blessing at the appropriate time" (NLT).

What does God guarantee will happen if we keep following and remain faithful? How does this encourage you?

Encounters

"God's greatest blessings often come costumed as disasters." (p. 145)

REMINDERS

With Jesus, it is *never* too late.

- Our "next door Savior" loves to surprise us with fresh starts and new horizons.
- To experience God's best, we must have Christ "in the boat" with us.
- To experience God's best, we have to go obediently to places we've never been and do things we've never done.
- Christ doesn't abandon those who have failed or "blown it." Quite the contrary, he enlists them.

6

Spit Therapy

Suffering People

"Talk about a thankless role. Selected to suffer. Some sing to God's glory. Others teach to God's glory. Who wants to be blind for God's glory? Which is tougher—the condition or discovering it was God's idea?" (pp. 43–44)

IMPRESSIONS

Try to summarize the main idea of chapter 6 in *Next Door Savior* in fifty words or less. What's the story? What are the lessons you see?

Have you ever witnessed what you would regard as a bona fide miracle? What? How did it affect you then? Now?

Of all the things the Bible says Jesus *did,* what amazes you most? What troubles you most? What surprises you most?

The "big idea" permeating the pages of *Next Door Savior* is that Jesus Christ is fully God and fully man. Divinity and humanity inseparably united in one person forever. How is this extraordinary claim of Christianity different from the claims of all the other world religions?

Remember the prayer of the psalm writer: "Open my eyes to see the wonderful truths in your law" (Psalm 119:18 NLT)? Ask God to give *you* keen spiritual vision as you examine the words and works of Christ in this chapter of the guidebook.

GLIMPSES

A great picture of how God deals with suffering people is found in John 9:1–38. There we find the account of Jesus, our next door Savior, healing a man who had been born blind.

As He passed by, He saw a man blind from birth. And His disciples asked Him, "Rabbi, who sinned, this man or his parents, that he would be born blind?" Jesus answered, "It was neither that this man sinned, nor his parents; but it was so that the works of God might be displayed in him. We must work the works of Him who sent Me as long as it is day; night is coming when no one can work. While I am in the world, I am the Light of the world." When He had said this, He spat on the ground, and made clay of the spittle, and applied the clay to his eyes, and said to him, "Go, wash in the pool of Siloam" (which is translated, Sent). So he went away and washed, and came back seeing.

Therefore the neighbors, and those who previously saw him as a beggar, were saying, "Is not this the one who used to sit and beg?" Others were saying, "This is he," still others were saying, "No, but he is like him." He kept saying, "I am the one." So they were saying to him, "How then were your eyes opened?" He answered, "The man who is called Jesus made clay, and anointed my eyes, and said to me, 'Go to Siloam and wash'; so I went away and washed, and I received sight." They said to him, "Where is He?" He said, "I do not know."

They brought to the Pharisees the man who was formerly blind. Now it was a Sabbath on the day when Jesus made the clay and opened his eyes. Then the Pharisees also were asking him again how he received his sight. And he said to them, "He applied clay to my eyes, and I washed, and I see." Therefore some of the Pharisees were saying, "This man is not from God, because He does not keep the Sabbath." But others were saying, "How can a man who is a sinner perform such signs?" And there was a division among them. So they said to the blind man again, "What do you say about Him, since He opened your eyes?" And he said, "He is a prophet." The Jews then did not believe it of him, that he had been blind and had received sight, until they called the parents of the very one who had received his sight, and questioned them, saying, "Is this your son, who you say was born blind? Then how does he now see?"

His parents answered them and said, "We know that this is our son, and that he was born blind; but how he now sees, we do not know; or who opened his eyes, we do not know. Ask him; he is of age, he will speak for himself." His parents said this because they were afraid of the Jews; for the Jews had already agreed that if anyone confessed Him to be Christ, he was to be put out of the synagogue. For this reason his parents said, "He is of age; ask him."

Encounters

"Yours is the hand he loves to hold." (p. 31)

So a second time they called the man who had been blind, and said to him, "Give glory to God; we know that this man is a sinner." He then answered, "Whether He is a sinner, I do not know; one thing I do know, that though I was blind, now I see." So they said to him, "What did He do to you? How did He open your eyes?" He answered them, "I told you already and you did not listen; why do you want to hear it again? You do not want to become His disciples too, do you?"

They reviled him and said, "You are His disciple, but we are disciples of Moses. "We know that God has spoken to Moses, but as for this man, we do not know where He is from." The man answered and said to them, "Well, here is an amazing thing, that you do not know where He is from, and yet He opened my eyes. We know that God does not hear sinners; but if anyone is God-fearing and does His will, He hears him. Since the beginning of time it has never been heard that anyone opened the eyes of a person born blind. If this man were not from God, He could do nothing." They answered him, "You were born entirely in sins, and are you teaching us?" So they put him out.

Jesus heard that they had put him out, and finding him, He said, "Do you believe in the Son of Man?" He answered, "Who is He, Lord, that I may believe in Him?" Jesus said to him, "You have both seen Him, and He is the one who is talking with you." And he said, "Lord, I believe." And he worshiped Him.

What five adjectives would describe your gut level response to this miracle of Christ?

Max writes: "The world abounds with paintings of . . . Jesus weeping, laughing, teaching, . . . but I've never seen a painting of Jesus spitting." That's an intriguing thought. We are accustomed to think of Christ healing and teaching—even walking on water. But spitting? Does that seem crude to you? How does this picture compare with how you've previously viewed Christ?

Jesus could have spoken a word, or touched the man's eyes (as he had done for so many other sick people on so many other occasions). But this time he spit, mixed the saliva with dust to make a handful of clay, and smeared the muddy concoction on—perhaps even in!—the blind man's eyes. It's a bizarre turn of events, because if you're already having difficulty seeing, an eye full of mud isn't likely to make your situation better!

Encounters

_____

_____

_____

_____

_____

_____

_____

_____

_____

_____

_____

_____

_____

_____

_____

_____

"There is a look that says, 'It's too late.'" (p. 35)

Are you surprised by Jesus' actions? What does this unexpected act suggest about our tendency to try to figure God out or put him in a box?

Describe the various eyewitness reactions to this miracle:

- The response of the man's parents

- The response of the man's neighbors

- The response of the disciples

- The response of the Pharisees and religious leaders

- The response of the man himself

> "Our task on earth is singular—to choose our eternal home. You can afford many wrong choices in life. You can choose the wrong career and survive, the wrong city and survive, the wrong house and survive. You can even choose the wrong mate and survive. But there is one choice that must be made correctly, and that is your eternal destiny."
>
> —AND THE ANGELS WERE SILENT

Why do you think there wasn't instant, unanimous joy regarding this astounding marvel?

Encounters

"Do you have any worn, wet, empty nets?" (p. 37)

What does Jesus mean when he refers to himself as the "Light of the world" (v. 5)? What does light do? How is it indispensable?

MUSINGS

What was the immediate assumption of the disciples when they came upon this blind man? Does this kind of thinking persist in modern culture? How about you? Do *you* view personal setbacks and suffering as God's punishment? Why or why not?

Why, when hard times or tragedies strike, are we so quick to ask "Why?"? In your opinion, or better yet, in your *experience*, does God often provide *reasons* for the trials in our lives?

Suppose God *did* give each of us a personalized explanation for each sorrow and time of suffering—would that make our pain go away? In other words, can a head full of answers really soothe a heart filled with pain?

How can God get glory from a handicap or disease? What if a sickness never goes away? Isn't he most honored when people are healed? (Hint: See 2 Corinthians 12.)

Ironically, the blind man's healing brought him a whole new set of problems. Suddenly, shockingly, his family and his "church" viciously turned on him. But "Jesus heard that they had thrown him out, and went and found him" (v. 35, MSG).

What does this act of Christ teach you about the heart of God? What does this suggest about those occasions in which you are troubled?

Encounters

"He knows your nets are empty. He knows your heart is weary." (p. 37)

DECISIONS

"This book will be held by arthritic hands. These chapters will be read by tear-filled eyes. Some of your legs are wheelchaired, and your hearts are hope starved. But 'these hard times are small potatoes compared to the coming good times, the lavish celebration prepared for us' (2 Corinthians 4:17 MSG)." (p. 46)

How does the guarantee of heaven and the promise of eternal reward help us face the great struggles of this life? How would you answer the person who said, "Aw, that's just escapist, pie-in-the-sky type thinking!"?

Are you suffering today? Perhaps battling some kind of physical affliction? Let there be no doubt that Jesus has the power to heal your body. Completely. Instantly. Yet, for reasons known only to heaven, he may choose *not* to do so. For what other miracles—besides a clean bill of health from your doctor—could you trust God in your current condition? How can the works of God be displayed in you, no matter what?

What are some specific, practical, loving actions you can take today for someone you know who is suffering?

A few rare souls face terrible hardship with great dignity and grace. They do not complain. In fact, they actually minister *out of their pain* to those with whom they come in contact. Many, however, become filled with self-pity and bitterness. They complain non-stop.

How do we develop the kind of Christlike character that is able to take suffering in stride and continues to be a blessing to others?

Encounters

_____

_____

_____

_____

_____

_____

_____

_____

_____

_____

_____

_____

_____

_____

_____

_____

_____

"Heaven gave earth her finest gift.
The Lamb of God who took away the sin of the world." (p. 142)

Memorize Romans 8:28 (NLT):

And we know that God causes everything to work together for the good of those who love God and are called according to his purpose for them.

How does this truth relate to what you have been studying here?

REMINDERS

- Suffering is a great mystery and hardship, but God can and will use it to bring glory to himself.
- Jesus cares deeply for us when we hurt—in fact he seeks us out to show us his love.
- When we are able to focus on Jesus, we somehow forget about ourselves and our troubles, and we bow in worship.

7
What Jesus Says at Funerals

Grieving People

"There is a time to say nothing. Your words can't dispel a fog, but your presence can warm it. And your words can't give a Lazarus back to his sisters. But God's can. And it's just a matter of time before he speaks. 'The Lord himself will come down from heaven with a commanding shout. . . . All the Christians who have died will rise from their graves'" (1 Thessalonians 4:16, NLT). (p. 54)

IMPRESSIONS

Chapter 7 of *Next Door Savior* gives us a fascinating insider's glimpse of Jesus at the funeral of one of his best friends. Have you read these four pages yet? If not, take a few moments now to skim back over the scene. There's a lot here to ponder, much life-changing truth to be gleaned.

What is the most uplifting and God-honoring funeral you've ever attended? What made it so hopeful?

What is the most depressing funeral you've ever witnessed? What made it difficult to sit through?

This is not an attempt to be morbid, but your time on earth could come to an end at any moment. When that happens, some grief-stricken relative or stunned friend will begin making phone calls to take care of all the arrangements. Here's your chance: What would *you* like your funeral service to be like—in tone, content, and so forth? How would you like the memorial to unfold? Are there any special songs you'd like sung? What people would you select to be your pallbearers? What sentiments or messages would you want expressed to your gathered friends and family members?

Yes, the mortality rate has been the same since the days of Adam: one death for every person. Even though death *is* a universal certainty, it's the experience for which many people are unprepared. Pray and ask God to give you his perspective. Ask him to answer your questions and calm your fears—so that you might be able to comfort others who grieve.

GLIMPSES

John 11 offers us some amazing insights into death and life. Most importantly, it shows us the power and compassion of our next door Savior when grief comes calling.

A man named Lazarus was sick. He lived in Bethany with his sisters, Mary and Martha. This is the Mary who poured the expensive perfume on the Lord's feet and wiped them with her hair. Her brother, Lazarus, was sick. So the two sisters sent a message to Jesus telling him, "Lord, the one you love is very sick." But when Jesus heard about it he said, "Lazarus's sickness will not end in death. No, it is for the glory of God. I, the Son of God, will receive glory from this." Although Jesus loved Martha, Mary, and Lazarus, he stayed where he was for the next two days and did not go to them.

Finally after two days, he said to his disciples, "Let's go to Judea again." But his disciples objected. "Teacher," they said, "only a few days ago the Jewish leaders in Judea were trying to kill you. Are you going there again?" Jesus replied, "There are twelve hours of daylight every day. As long as it is light, people can walk safely. They can see because they have the light of this world. Only at night is there danger of stumbling because there is no light." Then he said, "Our friend

> "A repentant heart is all he demands. Come out of the shadows! Be done with your hiding! A repentant heart is enough to summon the Son of God himself to walk through our walls of guilt and shame. . . . All we have to do is come back. No wonder they call him the Savior."
>
> —NO WONDER THEY CALL HIM THE SAVIOR

Lazarus has fallen asleep, but now I will go and wake him up." The disciples said, "Lord, if he is sleeping, that means he is getting better!" They thought Jesus meant Lazarus was having a good night's rest, but Jesus meant Lazarus had died. Then he told them plainly, "Lazarus is dead. And for your sake, I am glad I wasn't there, because this will give you another opportunity to believe in me. Come, let's go see him." Thomas, nicknamed the Twin, said to his fellow disciples, "Let's go, too—and die with Jesus."

Encounters

"It's not too late to try again." (p. 37)

When Jesus arrived at Bethany, he was told that Lazarus had already been in his grave for four days. Bethany was only a few miles down the road from Jerusalem, and many of the people had come to pay their respects and console Martha and Mary on their loss. When Martha got word that Jesus was coming, she went to meet him. But Mary stayed at home. Martha said to Jesus, "Lord, if you had been here, my brother would not have died. But even now I know that God will give you whatever you ask." Jesus told her, "Your brother will rise again." "Yes," Martha said, "when everyone else rises, on resurrection day." Jesus told her, "I am the resurrection and the life. Those who believe in me, even though they die like everyone else, will live again. They are given eternal life for believing in me and will never perish. Do you believe this, Martha?" "Yes, Lord," she told him. "I have always believed you are the Messiah, the Son of God, the one who has come into the world from God." Then she left him and returned to Mary. She called Mary aside from the mourners and told her, "The Teacher is here and wants to see you." So Mary immediately went to him. Now Jesus had stayed outside the village, at the place where Martha met him. When the people who were at the house trying to console Mary saw her leave so hastily, they assumed she was going to Lazarus's grave to weep. So they followed her there. When Mary arrived and saw Jesus, she fell down at his feet and said, "Lord, if you had been here, my brother would not have died."

When Jesus saw her weeping and saw the other people wailing with her, he was moved with indignation and was deeply troubled. "Where have you put him?" he asked them. They told him, "Lord, come and see." Then Jesus wept. The people who were standing nearby said, "See how much he loved him." But some said, "This man healed a blind man. Why couldn't he keep Lazarus from dying?" And again Jesus was deeply troubled. Then they came to the grave. It was a cave with a stone rolled across its entrance. "Roll the stone aside," Jesus told them. But Martha, the dead man's sister, said, "Lord, by now the smell will be terrible because he has been dead for four days." Jesus responded, "Didn't I tell you that you will see God's glory if you believe?" So they rolled the stone aside. Then Jesus looked up to heaven and said, "Father, thank you for hearing me. You always hear me, but I said it out loud for the sake of all these people standing here, so they will believe you sent me." Then Jesus shouted, "Lazarus, come out!" And Lazarus came out, bound in graveclothes, his face wrapped in a headcloth. Jesus told them, "Unwrap him and let him go!" (NLT)

"Friends send Christ an urgent appeal in a humble fashion, and what does he do? 'He stayed where he was for the next two days and did not go to them' (v. 6 NLT)." (p. 52)

Why do you think Jesus stayed and didn't leave right away? Nothing in these verses indicates that Jesus had life-and-death business to tend to in the place he was when he got the word about his beloved friend, Lazarus; yet he seemed to dilly-dally there? Why didn't Jesus immediately set out for Bethany?

Encounters

"Trace this condition back to heaven. The reason the man was born sightless? So 'the works of God might be displayed in him.'" (p. 43)

If you had been one of Christ's disciples, what would you have made of his cryptic words about Lazarus in the second paragraph above (verses 4–16)?

What various words and phrases are used to describe Jesus' reaction to the events of John 11?

Put yourself among the mourners and witnesses and family members described above. What would be your opinion of Jesus at events described at the beginning of the chapter? At the end?

How do the following passages describe our brief time on the earth?

James 4:14:

Psalm 39:4–6:

Psalm 102:11:

Psalm 103:15–16:

> "Jesus. The man. A bronzed Galilean who spoke with such thunderous authority and loved with such childlike humility. The God. The one who claimed to be older than time and greater than death. "
>
> —GOD CAME NEAR

Encounters

"If there be any doubt regarding God's full-bore devotion, he does things like this. He tracks down a troubled pauper." (p. 46)

MUSINGS

"Jesus . . . weeps. He sits on the pew between Mary and Martha, puts an arm around each, and sobs. Among the three, a tsunami of sorrow is stirred; a monsoon of tears is released. Tears that reduce to streaks the watercolor conceptions of a cavalier Christ. Jesus weeps. He weeps with them. He weeps for them. He weeps with you. He weeps for you. He weeps so we will know: Mourning is not disbelieving. Flooded eyes don't represent a faithless heart." (p. 53)

How does this image of Christ—with tears cascading down his cheeks—change your perspective on grief?

What does healthy grief look like? How, specifically, does it differ from unbiblical despair?

What does it mean—what does it look like—to grieve without hope (see 1 Thessalonians 4:13)?

The question really isn't "*Will* death visit me and my loved ones?" but "*When* will death visit me and my loved ones?" What about you? Are you ready? (Not necessarily *eager*, but ready for eternity?) Have you made peace with God?

As much as possible, as far as it depends on you, have you attempted to make peace with all the people God has put in your life (Romans 12:18)?

Encounters

"Just as he came for the blind man, Jesus is coming for you. The hand that touched the blind man's shoulder will touch your cheeks. The face that changed his life will change yours." (p. 47)

DECISIONS

"A person can enter a cemetery Jesus—certain of life after death and still have a Twin Tower crater in the heart. Christ did. He wept, and he knew he was ten minutes from seeing a living Lazarus!" (p. 53)

If you found yourself in the throes of deep grief, which of the following people (if any) would you most want to see coming? Why?

- the well-meaning friend who keeps telling you not to be sad
- the person who keeps insisting, "I know exactly how you feel!"
- the neighbor who quotes Bible verses and Christian sayings
- the fellow church member who sends numerous e-mails filled with inspirational stories
- the aunt who sits with you in silence and just hugs you and cries with you
- the co-worker who offers you a number of books and taped sermons on grief
- the small group member who just lets you vent (without judging your anger or sadness), and who just really listens to your heart
- the person who changes the subject every time you bring up your grief

Romans 12:15 commands Christians: "Rejoice with those who rejoice; mourn with those who mourn" (NIV).

How, specifically, do we put this verse into practice? What people in your life are weeping and sorrowful?

It's always difficult to know what to say to those who have lost a loved one. What do you typically say? How do you act? How do you normally try to comfort the bereaved?

Encounters

"*Search the crucifixion sky for one ray of hope, and you won't find it.*" (p. 146)

What *is* the ultimate answer or solution for deep grief? Where and how do we find true healing?

REMINDERS

- Christ weeps with us and for us when we are grieving.
- It is *not* a sign of disbelief to grieve the loss of a loved one. Jesus grieved deeply the death of Lazarus.
- Jesus has personally tasted *and* conquered death. In fact, he is "the resurrection and the life" (John 11:25)!
- In the same way that Christ raised Lazarus from the dead, he will one day raise all who are dead in Christ. He has the final say about death!

8

Getting the Hell Out

Tormented People

"Our enemy has a complex and conniving spiritual army. . . . But . . . in God's presence, the devil is a wimp. Satan is to God what a mosquito is to an atomic bomb." (pp. 58–59)

IMPRESSIONS

Have you read chapter 8 of *Next Door Savior*? If not, take a few minutes now to do so.

What do you think the Spirit of God wants you to see here—about Jesus, about the devil, about living in a fallen world, about people who are under the control of the evil one?

What thoughts or images come to mind when you hear someone mention "Satan"?

The great British thinker/author C. S. Lewis once wrote: "There are two equal and opposite errors into which our race can fall about the devils. One is to disbelieve in their existence. The other is to believe, and to feel an excessive and unhealthy interest in them."

Would those who know you best say *you* tend toward one of these errors? Which one?

What evidence might you present to convince to a skeptical friend that Satan *is* alive and well on the earth?

As you begin the process of wrestling through the vital concepts in this chapter, pay careful attention to these words of the apostle Paul:

A final word: Be strong with the Lord's mighty power. Put on all of God's armor so that you will be able to stand firm against all strategies and tricks of the Devil. For we are not fighting against people made of flesh and blood, but against the evil rulers and authorities of the unseen world, against those mighty powers of darkness who rule this world, and against wicked spirits in the heavenly realms. Use every piece of God's armor to resist the enemy in the time of evil, so that after the battle you will still be standing firm. (Ephesians 6:10–13 NLT)

Then ask God for eyes to see and understand his truth and a heart of compassion and courage to help others find real freedom living by his truth.

GLIMPSES

Mark 5:2–20 (NLT)

Just as Jesus was climbing from the boat, a man possessed by an evil spirit ran out from a cemetery to meet him. This man lived among the tombs and could not be restrained, even with a chain. Whenever he was put into chains and shackles—as he often was—he snapped the chains from his wrists and smashed the shackles. No one was strong enough to control him. All day long and throughout the night, he would wander among the tombs and in the hills, screaming and hitting himself with stones.

When Jesus was still some distance away, the man saw him. He ran to meet Jesus and fell down before him. He gave a terrible scream, shrieking, "Why are you bothering me, Jesus, Son of the Most High God? For God's sake, don't torture me!" For Jesus had already said to the spirit, "Come out of the man, you evil spirit."

Then Jesus asked, "What is your name?"

And the spirit replied, "Legion, because there are many of us here inside this man." Then the spirits begged him again and again not to send them to some distant place. There happened to be a large herd of pigs feeding on the hillside nearby.

"Send us into those pigs," the evil spirits begged. Jesus gave them permission. So the evil spirits came out of the man and entered the pigs, and the entire herd of two thousand pigs plunged down the steep hillside into the lake, where they drowned.

The herdsmen fled to the nearby city and the surrounding countryside, spreading the news as they ran. Everyone rushed out to see for themselves. A crowd soon gathered around Jesus, but they were frightened when they saw the man who had been demon possessed, for he was sitting there fully clothed and perfectly sane. Those who had seen what happened to the man and to the pigs told everyone about it, and the crowd began pleading with Jesus to go away and leave them alone.

When Jesus got back into the boat, the man who had been demon possessed begged to go, too. But Jesus said, "No, go home to your friends, and tell them what wonderful things the Lord has done for

Encounters

_____

_____

_____

_____

_____

_____

_____

_____

_____

_____

_____

_____

_____

_____

_____

_____

"Who was really blind that day? The neighbors didn't see the man; they saw a novelty. The church leaders didn't see the man; they saw a technicality. The parents didn't see their son; they saw a social difficulty. In the end, no one saw him." (p. 45)

you and how merciful he has been." So the man started off to visit the Ten Towns of that region and began to tell everyone about the great things Jesus had done for him; and everyone was amazed at what he told them.

In what specific ways did Satan torment this man?

What is the significance of the name "Legion"? (Hint: See page 58 of *Next Door Savior.*)

Describe the radical change in this man after Jesus delivered him from his demonic possession/oppression.

What lessons do the following Bible passages teach us about the devil and engaging in spiritual warfare?

Genesis 3:1–5

Matthew 4:1

Mark 1:27

John 8:44

John 10:10

2 Corinthians 11:14

James 4:7

1 Peter 5:8

1 John 4:4

> Signs that a Person May
> Be Under the Strong
> Influence of Satan:
>
> Self-inflicted pain
>
> Obsession with death and
> darkness
>
> Endless restlessness
>
> Isolation

Encounters

"Grief fogs in the heart like a Maine-coast morning." (p. 52)

MUSINGS

Referring to this tormented man, Mark 5:4 notes that "no one was strong enough to subdue him." No one, that is, until Jesus crossed his path. Jesus showed up, and love won the day. Love not only covers a multitude of sins (1 Peter 4:8), it also conquers the *power* of sin.

When in your life have you been most overpowered or overwhelmed by the love of Christ? What happened?

Mark 5:5 (AMP) says that this demon-possessed man was "always . . . bruising himself with stones." He was physically self-destructive. Max writes: "We are more sophisticated; we use drugs, sex, work, violence and food" (p. 58). Or how about the way some people jump from one bad relationship to another without ever seeming to learn?

In what ways, if any, has Satan successfully managed to get *you* to shoot yourself in the foot spiritually, emotionally, relationally, or physically? Would those who know you best and love you most say that you are hurting yourself in some way? What way? How?

This poor man was in *spiritual* bondage and the solution of some was to try to bind him *physically!* The plan failed, and the man remained in torment. What have been some of the futile solutions you've tried to apply to the problems in your life?

"How else do we explain our bizarre behavior? The violent rages of a father. The secret binges of a mother. The sudden rebellion of a teenager. Maxed-out credit cards. Internet pornography. Satan does not sit still. A glimpse of the wild man [in Mark 5:2–20] reveals Satan's goal for you and me." (p. 57)

What would you say to those who argue that this kind of thinking is giving the devil too much credit? Or that it is trying to shift the blame off of ourselves?

Encounters

"Every funeral has its Marthas.
Sprinkled among the bereaved are the bewildered." (p. 52)

How can intimate fellowship with other Christians help foil the work of the evil one in our lives?

> "Sense Jesus's power. Blind eyes . . . seeing. Fruitless tree . . . withering. Money changers . . . scampering. Religious leaders . . . cowering. Tomb . . . opening. Hear his promise. Death has no power. Failure holds no prisoners. Fear has no control. For God has come, God has come into your world . . . to take you home."
>
> —AND THE ANGELS WERE SILENT

DECISIONS

"The punch line of the passage is Jesus' power over Satan. One word from Christ, and the demons are swimming with the swine, and the wild man is 'clothed and in his right mind' (Mark 5:13, 15). Just one command!" (p. 60)

Ephesians 4:27 warns against giving the devil a foothold in our lives. How might we allow this? (Hint: Note the immediate context of that command and the sins that are being warned against in the verses just proceeding.

Do you personally feel tormented in any way right now? Under spiritual attack? Helpless? Defeated by a certain sin? Describe your struggle in the space below:

What Christian friend (or pastor or counselor) do you trust enough to share your deep struggles?

Toward the end of Paul's most often quoted chapter on the subject of spiritual warfare, he writes:

And pray in the Spirit on all occasions with all kinds of prayers and requests. With this in mind, be alert and always keep on praying for all the saints (Ephesians 6:18 NIV).

Encounters

"*Mourning is not disbelieving. Flooded eyes don't represent a faithless heart.*" (p. 53)

In light of what you've studied here about the devil and spiritual warfare, how do your prayers for yourself need to change? What about your prayers for your fellow Christians?

REMINDERS

- The devil is the bitter enemy of our souls, and he seeks to not only torment us but also destroy our lives.

- Those who are in Christ do not have to fear the evil one; he has been defeated by the death and resurrection of Jesus.

- Though we are *confident* (of Christ's absolute and ultimate victory over Satan), we must be *careful* (of Satan's still-potent power). The devil can disturb us, but he cannot defeat us.

9
It's Not Up to You

Spiritually Weary People

"God doesn't send us to obedience school to learn new habits, he sends us to the hospital to be given a new heart. Forget training, he gives transplants." (p. 66)

IMPRESSIONS

Chapter 9 of *Next Door Savior* introduces us to some radical spiritual concepts. Unfortunately many people have never even heard—much less understood—these transforming truths. Take a few minutes to refresh your memory. Look back over pages 65–70 of *Next Door Savior*. (Note: They focus on a late night conversation between a Jewish religious scholar named Nicodemus and Jesus.)

What ideas or statements here stand out?

What thoughts in this chapter surprise you or seem dubious to you?

What statements don't you understand?

What images or notions are new to you?

Which of the following statements come close to describing what you have been taught it means to be acceptable to God? (Check all that apply).

_____ Do your best and hope that, in the end, your good deeds outweigh your mistakes.

_____ Learn God's rules and keep God's rules.

_____ Practice your religion—whatever it happens to be—consistently.

_____ Live a righteous life. Make it your goal to go about doing good.

_____ Attend church and follow the traditions of the church.

_____ Think constantly about God; live constantly for God.

_____ Make sacrifices for God and for others.

_____ Try to stop doing bad stuff and try to start doing good things.

_____ Allow God to make you into a brand-new person.

What is the problem with so many of these approaches?

How is the final statement different from all the rest?

Of all the statements Jesus ever *said,* which one amazes you most? What troubles you most? What surprises you most? What comforts you most?

Before you begin to work through this portion of the *Next Door Savior Guidebook,* pray this prayer from Ephesians 3:14–21 (adapted and modified from the NLT):

When I think of the wisdom and scope of God's plan, I fall to my knees and pray to the Father, the Creator of everything in heaven and on earth. I pray that from his glorious, unlimited resources he might give me mighty inner strength through his Holy Spirit. And I pray that Christ will be more and more at home in my heart as I trust in him. May my roots go down deep into the soil of God's marvelous love. And may I have the power to understand, as all God's people should, how wide, how long, how high, and how deep his love really is. May I experience the love of Christ, though it is so great I will never fully understand it. Then I will be filled with the fullness of life and power that comes from God. Now glory be to God! By his mighty power at work within me, he is able to accomplish infinitely more than I would ever dare to ask or hope. May he be given glory in the church and in Christ Jesus forever and ever through endless ages. Amen.

Encounters

"We know who has the final say about death." (p. 54)

GLIMPSES

John 3:1–6 (NLT)

After dark one evening, a Jewish religious leader named Nicodemus, a Pharisee, came to speak with Jesus. "Teacher," he said, "we all know that God has sent you to teach us. Your miraculous signs are proof enough that God is with you." Jesus replied, "I assure you, unless you are born again, you can never see the Kingdom of God." "What do you mean?" exclaimed Nicodemus. "How can an old man go back into his mother's womb and be born again?" Jesus replied, "The truth is, no one can enter the Kingdom of God without being born of water and the Spirit. Humans can reproduce only human life, but the Holy Spirit gives new life from heaven.

THE NEW COVENANT

The Old Testament book of Exodus details how God gave Moses his laws for Israel on tablets of stone. The rest of the Old Testament shows how the Jewish people tried in vain to obey these exacting rules for life. It was a frustrating, impossible system. No one kept the law perfectly. Daily, through the bloody sacrificial system, the people were reminded of their dismal failure to please God. Eventually, most folks lost heart and quit trying.

Hundreds of years later, speaking through the prophet Ezekiel, God hinted at a new arrangement to come: "I will give you a new heart with new and right desires, and I will put a new spirit in you. I will take out your stony heart of sin and give you a new, obedient heart. And I will put my Spirit in you so you will obey my laws and do whatever I command" (Ezekiel 36:26–27 NLT).

What a spectacular promise! In contrast with the Old Covenant's external list of laws, this "New Covenant" would involve internal transformation. Talk about exciting! God was promising a new plan that would change people from the inside out.

This was a prophecy Nicodemus should have known. And *this* is what Jesus meant when he spoke of the new birth. Fact is, when we put our trust in Jesus, a spiritual revolution takes place. Our sins are forgiven—fully and forever. We become new creatures in Christ (2 Corinthians 5:17). We are born again (or born from above, see John 3:3) as children of God (John 1:12). God takes up residence in our lives (Ephesians 1:13).

No longer do we have to try in vain to be good. Spiritually speaking, we have God's DNA within us—new hearts, new desires, and new power to live as God commands.

Encounters

"Dismiss any image of a red-suited Satan with a pitchfork and pointy tail.
The devil is a strong devil." (p. 59)

What do you know about the Pharisees? (Hint: See p. 66 of *Next Door Savior*.) Summarize their view of the spiritual life.

Why do you suppose Nicodemus came to Jesus at night?

Think about this man's devotion to the strict demands of his Pharisaical religion. Do you agree with Max's contention: "When it comes to life, he's tired. . . . Tired of rules and regulations but no rest. Nicodemus is looking for a change. And he has a hunch Jesus can give it" (pp. 66–67)? Take a shot at describing this man's soul, his daily existence. Do you picture a joyous man? Or an exhausted one? A guy filled with delight—or desperation?

What did Jesus mean when he abruptly told "Dr. Nick" he needed to be "born again"? What is involved in a spiritual rebirth in "new life from heaven"? How does a person get this life?

What do the following passages teach about spiritual transformation? What images or word pictures are used? What is God described as doing in each place?

Romans 6:1–14

Galatians 2:20

Ephesians 1:13

Philippians 1:6

Titus 3:4–7

> "It's the great triumph of heaven: God is on the earth. And it is the great tragedy of earth: man has rejected God."
>
> —AND THE ANGELS WERE SILENT

Encounters

"Hell makes us hurt ourselves." (p. 58)

MUSINGS

In what ways, if any, can you relate to Nicodemus?

In chapter 9, Max uses three analogies to explain God's amazing work within the soul of a believer:

- First, his dog Molly doing disgusting, dog-like things (for example, eating out of the garbage, drinking out of the toilet). The point? Molly does these things precisely because she *is* a dog; she has a dog's nature. Any change in her behavior would require a change in her essential nature.
- Second, his strenuous cleaning of a clunky old '65 Rambler station wagon. The point? The car looked and smelled better, but it ran just the same. It was still just a clunker.
- Third, the person who receives a heart transplant, exchanging a diseased heart for a healthy one. The point? Suddenly he or she can do things physically that were impossible before!

Which of these illustrations is most helpful to you in understanding the love and grace of God that is yours by virtue of the new birth?

How are the sincere religious efforts of millions of people worldwide really no different than giving an old jalopy a top-notch detailing job or slapping a fresh coat of paint on a termite-infested house?

Max writes: "Christ . . . gifts you with a finished work. He fulfilled the law for you. Bid farewell to the burden of religion. Gone is the fear that having done everything, you might not have done enough. You climb the stairs, not by your strength, but his. God pledges to help those who stop trying to help themselves" (p. 70).

If this is true, what do we say then to the oft-quoted statement, "God helps those who help themselves"?

Encounters

"In God's presence, the devil is a wimp." (p. 59)

If we really embrace the truths of the New Covenant—new birth, new life, a new nature, new desires, new power—it almost seems as though we would be able to live perfect lives! And yet, we each fail—many times daily. Why? What's the problem?

Here's Max's explanation for our continuing to sin:

"Did you exit the womb wearing cross-trainers? . . . Of course not. And when you started to walk, you fell more than you stood. Should we expect anything different from our spiritual walk? . . . The stumbles of a toddler do not invalidate the act of birth. And the stumbles of a Christian do not annul his spiritual birth. . . . Do you understand what God has done? He has deposited a Christ seed in you. As it grows, you will change. It's not that sin has no more presence in your life, but rather that sin has no more power over your life. Temptation will pester you, but temptation will not master you." (pp. 68–69)

What sins seem to trip *you* up most? How does the reality of the new birth give you new hope today in overcoming these old, bad habits?

DECISIONS

"Are you a Nicodemus? Religious as Saint Peter's Square, but feeling just as old? Pious, but powerless? If so, may I remind you of something?

"When you believe in Christ, Christ works a miracle in you. 'When you believed in Christ, he identified you as his own by giving you the Holy Spirit' (Eph. 1:13 NLT). You are permanently purified and empowered by God himself. The message of Jesus to the religious person is simple: It's not what you do. It's what I do. I have moved in. And in time you can say with Paul, 'I myself no longer live, but Christ lives in me' (Gal. 2:20 NLT). You are no longer a clunker, not even a clean clunker. You are a sleek Indianapolis Motor Speedway racing machine." (p. 68)

What specifically can you do this week to better live out the truths you've been studying in these pages?

Encounters

"Hell is an anthill against heaven's steamroller." (p. 60)

Someone has observed that religion is spelled D-O. In other words, it's all the stuff people think they have to *do* to earn God's approval. The problem is how do you know when or if you've done enough. And, what's even worse, every religion has a different to do list! No wonder so many devout people are so tired and so frustrated.

By contrast, Christianity is spelled D-O-N-E. It's the good news that Christ has already *done* everything needed to bring us into a right relationship with God. He died to pay for our sins. He rose to offer us a whole new kind of life. There is nothing for us to do except put our trust in Jesus. When we do, he moves in, and the transformation begins.

Have you ever invited Jesus to come into your life and change you from the inside out? Do you live like the old person or the new? Do you count yourself as having a new heart or old?

List the names of some friends or family members who still think that being religious is the formula for getting right with God.

Max insists, "You've got to test the new ticker. You've got to experiment with the new you." What would that look like in your life tomorrow? What are some simple ways you could begin to live in God's power? What are some things you could attempt that would definitely require you to depend on God's strength?

REMINDERS

- Jesus isn't interested in cosmetic changes to our lives; he wants to change us from the inside out.

- Real, lasting change always begins with the new birth.

- The new birth means we receive a new heart, a new nature, new desires, and a new power to live as we should. In short, we become brand new creatures (2 Corinthians 5:17).

- Spiritual growth, ultimately, is not dependent on us; maturity results when we trust God's Spirit to work within us and we step out in obedience.

10
The Trashman

Imperfect people

"His eyes compel her to step forward. He reaches for her trash and takes it from her. 'You can't live with this,' he explains. 'You weren't made to.' With head down, he empties her shame upon his shoulders. Then looking toward the heavens with tear-flooded eyes, he screams, 'I'm sorry!'" (p. 75)

IMPRESSIONS

Chapter 10 of *Next Door Savior* is a simple story, a modern-day parable. How did it make you feel when you first read it? Take a few minutes to read it again. Then, jot down your impressions in the spaces below:

I felt . . .

I realized . . .

I wondered . . .

I decided . . .

Most of the action in "The Trashman" takes place at a landfill. Ever been to one? How about a sewage treatment plant? What is the most repulsive place you've ever been? What made it so noxious and foul?

When did the gospel (the story of Jesus) become intensely personal and most real to you? Have you ever wept or come unglued while hearing about Christ's death on the cross for your sins—maybe during an Easter pageant or while taking the Lord's Supper or while watching a filmed version of the life of Christ? Perhaps while listening to a powerful hymn or sermon or beautiful praise chorus? What happened? How were you affected?

How long has it been since you were deeply moved by the message of the cross?

The problem with "the old, old story" of Christ is that, for church folk, it can become a little too familiar. We hear it expressed so often, that we become numb to its power and beauty. Ask God to give you a fresh appreciation for what he has done for you. Ask him to overwhelm you and to enlarge your heart as you reflect on the infinite love of our next door Savior. (Note: You might even wish to write out your story—how you first met Christ—on the next "Encounters" page.)

GLIMPSES

John 1 takes us back to the very beginning of Jesus' earthly ministry. John the Baptizer has been raised up by God to prepare people for the coming of the long-awaited Savior/Messiah. Dressed in camel skins and munching on a strange diet of wild locusts and honey, John has been preaching to huge crowds out in the desert near the Jordan River. John 1:29 (NIV) says:

> *"The next day John saw Jesus coming toward him and said, 'Look, the Lamb of God, who takes away the sin of the world!'"*

In his first public introduction, how is Jesus presented to the world? What is significant about John's calling Christ as "the Lamb of God, who takes away the sin of the world"?

Hundreds of years before this scene in John 1, another prophet by the name of Isaiah was moved by God to write these telling words:

Isaiah 53:6–12 (NLT)

All of us have strayed away like sheep. We have left God's paths to follow our own. Yet the LORD laid on him the guilt and sins of us all. He was oppressed and treated harshly, yet he never said a word. He was led as a lamb to the slaughter. And as a sheep is silent before the shearers, he did not open his mouth. From prison and trial they led him away to his death. But who among the people realized

Encounters

"To see the kingdom of God you need an unprecedented rebirth from God." (p. 67)

that he was dying for their sins—that he was suffering their punishment? He had done no wrong, and he never deceived anyone. But he was buried like a criminal; he was put in a rich man's grave.

But it was the LORD's good plan to crush him and fill him with grief. Yet when his life is made an offering for sin, he will have a multitude of children, many heirs. He will enjoy a long life, and the LORD's plan will prosper in his hands. When he sees all that is accomplished by his anguish, he will be satisfied. And because of what he has experienced, my righteous servant will make it possible for many to be counted righteous, for he will bear all their sins. I will give him the honors of one who is mighty and great, because he exposed himself to death. He was counted among those who were sinners. He bore the sins of many and interceded for sinners.

To whom was Isaiah referring? What would be the result of this sacrifice?

The apostle Paul, writing about the forgiveness and new life that God wants to give to everyone, and how such a miracle is even possible, expressed it this way: "For God made Christ, who never sinned, to be the offering for our sin, so that we could be made right with God through Christ" (2 Corinthians 5:21 NLT). Another translation renders that same verse with these words: "For He made Him who knew no sin to be sin for us, that we might become the righteousness of God in Him" (NKJV).

What do you think of that? The notion that Christ took all our sin upon himself and all the punishment that we deserve because of our rebellion, that he, in essence, became our sins? Is this a new thought to you?

MUSINGS

"She never looks at her trash. Early on she did. But what she saw repulsed her, so she's kept the sack closed ever since." (p. 73)

Chapter 10 pictures a variety of weary people dragging around large sacks of trash, and then meeting a kindly Trashman who offers to take their garbage. In what ways is a sack of trash, a big bag of garbage, a good metaphor for our sin and failure?

Someone has observed that behind every face there is a drama taking place. Ponder that truth: *every* person you meet is struggling with something. (And often several very large somethings!)

Encounters

"God gives no sponge baths. He washes us from head to toe." (p. 67)

How could grasping this truth alter the way you treat others?

To use the imagery of chapter 10, what would you say is in your "sack"? What are you dragging around? Regrets? Shame? Guilt? Anger? Rage? Fear? Bitterness? Selfishness? Possessiveness? How long have you had this burden? Aren't you sick of lugging it? Wouldn't you like to unload it?

Does the thought of Christ as a kind of trashman startle you? Does the thought of him taking away forever all your junk and baggage seem too simplistic and easy to you?

The film *The Mission* gives us a great picture of this truth. Actor Robert DeNiro plays a slave trader in South America who kills his brother in a fit of jealous rage. Overcome with guilt, he decides to forsake his evil profession and join a group of monks who are ministering to the very Indians he once enslaved.

In the movie's most powerful scene, in an effort to do penance for his sin, this grieving, tormented soul bundles up all the implements of his former life (his armor, sword, etc.), ties the giant sack to his shoulders and waist, and then begins to lug it all upriver, up into the mountains where the Indians live. It is grueling. Exhausting. Painful to watch him struggle with such an immense burden. Perhaps even more so because we see something of ourselves in his character.

When the ex-slave trader finally arrives in the village, he is instantly recognized. Weak and vulnerable, we expect him to be killed on the spot by a fierce-looking warrior with a machete. Shockingly, the Indian uses his weapon to cut away the big bundle of slave baggage; then he pushes it over the ledge. We watch, speechless, as these relics of the man's former life float back down the river, over the falls, and out of sight. DeNiro's character begins weeping uncontrollably with relief as he realizes he has been fully forgiven and freed from his terrible past.

Encounters

_____

_____

_____

_____

_____

_____

_____

_____

_____

_____

_____

_____

_____

_____

_____

_____

_____

"Your sins stand no chance against the fire hydrant of God's grace." (p. 67)

DECISIONS

When did you give your sack of garbage to Jesus Christ and let him deal with it? Describe that encounter. What happened? How did that experience change you?

> "Never were God's arms open so wide as they were on the Roman cross. One arm extending back into history and the other reaching into the future. An embrace of forgiveness offered for anyone who'll come. A hen gathering her chicks. A father receiving his own. A redeemer redeeming the world. No wonder they call him the Savior."
>
> —NO WONDER THEY CALL HIM THE SAVIOR

Perhaps, even as a Christian, you have begun filling a new sack or lugging an old one? One of the skills we have to learn as new believers is "claiming and utilizing the full forgiveness that is ours in Christ." Even though our desire is to follow Jesus, we will continue to sin, and we will continue to be sinned against. We need to be careful, for in those moments, the enemy sneaks up to our souls quietly. There he accuses and entices. He encourages us to pick up old bags of guilt and new bags of revenge and bitterness.

Can you think of some recent occasions when you realized this was taking place? Have you fallen back into the old habit of garbage-lugging?

In his book *Six Hours One Friday*, Max writes: "If we are not teaching people how to be saved, it is perhaps because we have forgotten the tragedy of being lost! If we're not teaching the message of forgiveness, it may be because we don't remember what it was like to be guilty. And if we're not preaching the cross, it could be that we've subconsciously decided that—God forbid—somehow we don't need it."

One way to recover the wonder and the joy of our amazing salvation is to make the effort to share the good news of Christ's love with those who don't yet know it. What people in your circle (neighbors, family members, coworkers, and others) still have never experienced the grace and forgiveness of Jesus?

Encounters

"God pledges to help those who stop trying to help themselves." (p. 70)

REMINDERS

- We all have sinned (Romans 3:23), yet none of us are equipped to deal with our sins.

- Lugging around our failures, mistakes, wrong choices, and regrets is exhausting.

- Christ came to take away the sins of the world— including *your* sins and mine!

- When we give Christ all our imperfection, he gives us his perfect standing with God!

11

He Loves to Be with the Ones He Loves

Every Place

"The God of the universe kicked against the wall of a womb, was born into the poverty of a peasant, and spent his first night in the feed trough of a cow. 'The Word became flesh and lived among us' (John 1:14 NRSV). The God of the universe left the glory of heaven and moved into the neighborhood. Our neighborhood! Who could have imagined he would do such a thing? Why? He loves to be with the ones he loves." (p. 85)

IMPRESSIONS

Review chapter 11 of *Next Door Savior*. It is barely three pages long, but it contains some powerful truths.

How did you feel as you were reading? What impressed you or surprised you or made you stop in mid-sentence?

This chapter begins with the observation: "Holiday time is highway time. Ever since Joseph and Mary packed their bags for Bethlehem, the birth of Jesus has caused people to hit the road. . . . 'tis the season to be traveling." Why *do* most of us go to such lengths (literally) to be with friends and family at Christmas time? What are some of your favorite holiday travel memories? What have been some of your most disastrous holiday journeys?

What do you like best about traveling? What's your preferred method of transportation? Favorite destination? What faraway place would you most like to visit and why?

A common view of God is that he sits aloof in the heavens. He is distant, remote, removed, untouchable. Some people refer to this belief system as "absentee landlord" theology. It's the notion that God erected the universe and then moved away. This kind of thinking says God is only vaguely interested in the affairs of earth. That he checks in only on rare occasions to collect the rent we owe him.

How would you convince an adherent of this position that the truth is otherwise?

> "The Omnipotent, in one instant, made himself breakable. . . . He who was larger than the universe became an embryo."
>
> —GOD CAME NEAR

There's a passage in the Old Testament book of Jeremiah that is noteworthy. In it, Jeremiah is expressing his hunger for God's Word, and the idea that he desperately needs God's truth to nourish his soul: "When your words came, I ate them; they were my joy and my heart's delight, for I bear your name, O LORD God Almighty" (Jeremiah 15:16 NIV). As you begin your time of reflection, ask God to give you a similar hunger for his Word. Tell the Lord you want to dine on his truth today!

GLIMPSES

"Holiday travel. It isn't easy. Then why do we do it? Why cram the trunks and endure the airports? You know the answer. We love to be with the ones we love. . . . So does God. . . . How else do you explain what he did?" (p. 84)

God *traveled*? He sure did. That very first Christmas. Jesus left heaven and came to earth—as a baby! Look at how the apostle Paul expresses it in Philippians 2:6–7: "Though he was God, he did not demand and cling to his rights as God. He made himself nothing; he took the humble position of a slave and appeared in human form" (NLT).

What does this tell you about Jesus? His nature? His love?

Encounters

"Oh, to be rid of this garbage." (p. 73)

The Bible doesn't ever give us a *comprehensive* look at heaven. We are, however, given occasional glimpses of that glorious place. Revelation 4:1–6a (NLT) is one such example. The apostle John writes:

> Then as I looked, I saw a door standing open in heaven, and the same voice I had heard before . . . said, "Come up here, and I will show you what must happen after these things." And instantly I was in the Spirit, and I saw a throne in heaven and someone sitting on it! The one sitting on the throne was as brilliant as gemstones—jasper and carnelian. And the glow of an emerald circled his throne like a rainbow. Twenty-four thrones surrounded him, and twenty-four elders sat on them. They were all clothed in white and had gold crowns on their heads. And from the throne came flashes of lightning and the rumble of thunder. And in front of the throne were seven lampstands with burning flames. They are the seven spirits of God. In front of the throne was a shiny sea of glass, sparkling like crystal.

Revelation 5:6–14 (NLT) continues this amazing description:

> I looked and I saw a Lamb that had been killed but was now standing between the throne and the four living beings and among the twenty-four elders. He had seven horns and seven eyes, which are the seven spirits of God that are sent out into every part of the earth. He stepped forward and took the scroll from the right hand of the one sitting on the throne. And as he took the scroll, the four living beings and the twenty-four elders fell down before the Lamb. Each one had a harp, and they held gold bowls filled with incense—the prayers of God's people!
>
> And they sang a new song with these words: "You are worthy to take the scroll and break its seals and open it. For you were killed, and your blood has ransomed people for God from every tribe and language and people and nation. And you have caused them to become God's Kingdom and his priests. And they will reign on the earth."
>
> Then I looked again, and I heard the singing of thousands and millions of angels around the throne and the living beings and the elders. And they sang in a mighty chorus: "The Lamb is worthy—the Lamb who was killed. He is worthy to receive power and riches and wisdom and strength and honor and glory and blessing."
>
> And then I heard every creature in heaven and on earth and under the earth and in the sea. They also sang: "Blessing and honor and glory and power belong to the one sitting on the throne and to the Lamb forever and ever."
>
> And the four living beings said, "Amen!" And the twenty-four elders fell down and worshiped God and the Lamb.

Encounters

"Will you give me your trash?" (p. 74)

What is revealed in these passages about heaven? How is it described? What is said here about Jesus Christ—the Lamb—and his place or position in heaven? How does this make his journey to earth on that first Christmas even more remarkable?

Take a few moments and think about the contrast between King Jesus, in glory in heaven, and baby Jesus, in a humble stable on earth. Write your impressions below:

MUSINGS

Max tells a moving story about a woman who volunteers to be disfigured like her husband, so that she can connect with him once again. How does this story affect you? How does it picture what Christ did for us?

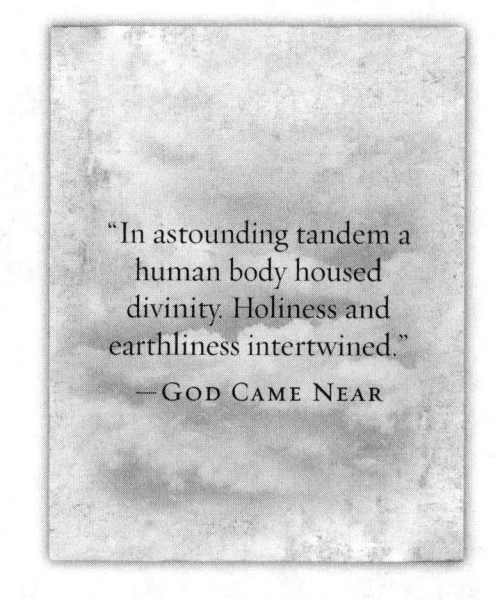

"In astounding tandem a human body housed divinity. Holiness and earthliness intertwined."
—GOD CAME NEAR

In the Old Testament, God spoke from a smoky mountaintop. Leading the nation of Israel through the wilderness and to the Promised Land, the Almighty was hidden in a cloud by day, and a pillar of fire by night. Take a minute to imagine what those experiences must have been like. How would these sights have impacted your view of God?

Encounters

"How could he know what he knew? And how could he know and still be so kind?" (p. 74)

In the New Testament, God spoke through a person. He took on humanity. He entered the world as a baby, and he grew to become a Galilean carpenter. In Jesus Christ, God became visible, vulnerable, approachable, touchable. If you could go back and witness any event, sermon, or miracle from the life of Jesus, what event would you choose and why?

How does the reality of Jesus, and the historicity of his life alter the way you view God? How *should* it affect his followers?

Think of the random people Jesus sought out and befriended: common tax collectors, immoral women, regular old Joe's (or Josephs). He sat with folks and ate. He laughed and hugged children. He healed the sick and stopped to converse with nobodies. If that sort of kindness and affection describes God for the brief moment in time he visited earth in the person of Jesus, what makes you think he views you any differently?

Imagine Jesus showing up at your place of work today. Based on what the Gospels show, what do you think Jesus might say to you?

DECISIONS

"He became like us. Just look at the places he was willing to go: feed troughs, carpentry shops, badlands, and cemeteries. . . . He loves to be with the ones he loves." (p.86)

Use one of the Encounters pages and write a letter of thanksgiving to God for the ultimate Christmas gift of Jesus Christ. Pour out your gratitude for what he has done for you. Express your deepest feelings to him.

Encounters

"Jesus orchestrated his final days to fulfill Old Testament prophecies." (p. 147)

Look around today. Study the people who pass by. How many of them do you think know—*really* know—that this is a God-visited, Christ-loved planet? If every Christian followed *your* example in sharing and spreading this amazing news, how many people would be hearing the news?

Jesus has returned physically to heaven, leaving his "body" (the Church) behind to show Christ to the world. How can your church do that better? What are some specific things you can do this week to demonstrate the reality of Jesus to those in your neighborhood?

REMINDERS

- God left heaven and journeyed to earth on that first Christmas.
- In becoming man, God humbled himself more than we can fathom.
- Christ did this, going to great trouble, because he loves to be with those he loves.
- One of the ones he loves is *you*!

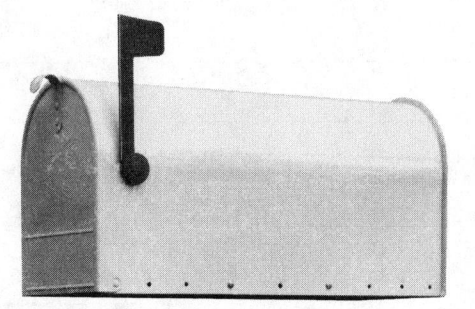

12
What's It Like?

Inward Places

"The first stop on his itinerary was a womb. Where will God go to touch the world? Look deep within Mary for an answer." (p. 90)

IMPRESSIONS

Four pages focused on one fantastic, faith-building fact—you *have* read chapter 12 of *Next Door Savior*, haven't you? If not, take a few minutes to do so now.

Well, what do you think of *that*? Are you stunned? Surprised? Encouraged? What is your first response to the reality of the indwelling Christ? He's even better than a next door Savior—he's a "live-in" one. He's the God who *moves in to your life* to stay!

Jot down your thoughts and reactions to this chapter in the space below (if you run out of room, don't forget the "Encounters" pages provided throughout this guidebook).

What character quality do you wish was more evident in your life? What character flaw would you love to be rid of?

What are three actions you know you probably ought to take and yet feel too powerless or ill-equipped to do so?

Because this chapter focuses primarily on Mary, the mother of Jesus, let's begin with some advice she once gave. It happened at a wedding in Cana, Galilee (you can find all the details in John 2). In short, some unexpected beverage issues arose, and the host of this big reception faced public embarrassment. He needed help, and fast!

Mary's counsel to the man's servants: "Do whatever [Jesus] tells you" (John 2:5 NLT).

That's good counsel for us too. As you begin this lesson, ask God to first make you able to *hear* what Jesus is trying to tell you. Then, and even more important, ask God for the courage and strength to *do* whatever he is leading you to do. And if, honestly, you don't feel very eager or excited, ask him to make you so. Pray something like this: "Lord, I'm not sure I want to do this, but I *want to want to*. Help me—change me, please."

GLIMPSES

Luke 1 records the extraordinary experience of Mary when she was visited by the angel Gabriel. The angel brought the mind-boggling news that she would be the mother of the long-awaited Messiah. How do you think she felt? What thoughts and questions must have been tumbling about in her mind?

Her response to the angel's news is found in Luke 1:38: "Mary responded, 'I am the Lord's servant, and I am willing to accept whatever he wants. May everything you have said come true'" (NLT). What stands out to you about her reaction? How do you think *you* might have answered?

Read and reflect on the following Bible verses:

"I am in you." (John 14:20 NCV*)*

". . . that Christ may dwell in your hearts through faith." (Ephesians 3:17 NIV*)*

". . . Christ in you, the hope of glory." (Colossians 1:27 NIV*)*

"Those who obey his commands live in him, and he in them." (1 John 3:24 NIV*)*

"Here I am! I stand at the door and knock. If anyone hears my voice and opens the door, I will come in and eat with him, and he with me." (Revelation 3:20 NIV*)*

What's the common theme in these Bible passages?

With this in mind, take a few moments to further reflect on Galatians 2:20 (NLT):

Encounters

"I'm tired of anger. He said he'd take it. . . . I'm going to give it to him." (p. 75)

"I myself no longer live, but Christ lives in me. So I live my life in this earthly body by trusting in the Son of God, who loved me and gave himself for me."

MUSINGS

Imagine taking a beginner's art class, and imagine your teacher assigning you this homework project: "Paint a Rembrandt-like masterpiece." Fat chance, right? But suppose, just as you were setting up your easel and getting out your palette, the "spirit of Rembrandt" (with all his artistic powers) somehow entered your body and, using *your* hands and eyes and fingers, began painting *through* you. What would happen? Your canvas might not look *exactly* like the master's, but don't you know it would be something to behold! Fellow class members would "ooh" and "ahh." Rembrandt's genius would be visible in *your* brushstrokes.

How, if at all, does this analogy help you understand the implications of "Christ in you, the hope of glory"?

> "Jesus was human. He wants us to know that he, too, knew the drone of the humdrum and the weariness that comes with long days. He wants us to remember that our trailblazer didn't wear bulletproof vests or rubber gloves or an impenetrable suit of armor. No, he pioneered our salvation through the world that you and I face daily."
>
> —NO WONDER THEY CALL HIM THE SAVIOR

Max writes: "Can't stop drinking? Christ can. And he lives within you. Can't stop worrying? Christ can. And he lives within you. Can't forgive the jerk, forget the past, or forsake your bad habits? Christ can! And he lives within you" (p. 91). What personal struggles and life issues do you seem to be powerless against right now?

Max writes: "What he did with Mary, he offers to us! He issues a Mary-level invitation to all his children. 'If you'll let me, I'll move in!'" (p. 90). Have *you* ever let Christ move in? Has there been a definite point in time when you heard Jesus knocking and when you opened the door and ushered him into your life? If so, what was that experience like? How has it changed you?

Encounters

"Why did Jesus travel so far?" (p. 84)

If Christ *is* in your life, does he inhabit *all* of it? Have you given him access to every place? Or have you refused to let him enter certain parts? On a scale of 1-10 (with 1= "He is pretty much invisible," and 10 = "He is the focus here, the center of attention"), rate his influence in the following areas of your life.

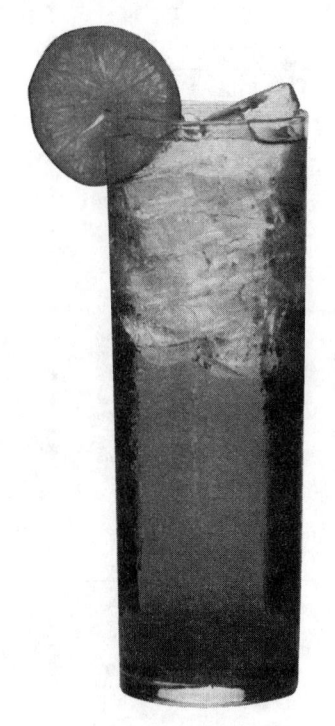

My thoughts

My words

My family interactions

My social life

My leisure time

My work

My use of money

My service to neighbors, the needy, etc.

My church involvement

Speaking to all those who have put their trust in Christ, Max writes: "[He] is *in* you. You are a modern-day Mary. Even more so. He was a fetus in her, but he is a force in you. He will do what you cannot. Imagine a million dollars being deposited into your checking account. To any observer you look the same, except for the goofy smile, but are you? Not at all! With God *in* you, you have a million resources that you did not have before!" (p. 91).

What are some of the implications of this reality? What are some tough situations you need to tackle with the "million resources" Christ has brought into your life?

DECISIONS

"We tend to assist God, assuming our part is as important as his. Or we resist, thinking we are too bad or too busy. Yet when we assist or resist, we miss God's great grace.

Encounters

*"Between him and us there was a distance—a great span.
And he couldn't bear it. . . . So he did something about it."* (p. 84)

We miss out on the reason we were placed on earth—to be so pregnant with heaven's child that he lives through us." (p. 92)

We cannot change ourselves, but we obviously do have to allow God to change us. What does that look like in everyday terms? Let's say one of your struggles is impatience. How, in an extremely trying situation, complete with frayed nerves and annoying people, does Christ live through you?

What do *you* need to do in those tempting moments? What is Jesus' role?

"Christ grew in Mary until he had to come out. Christ will grow in you until the same occurs. He will come out in your speech, in your actions, in your decisions. Every place you live will be a Bethlehem, and every day you live will be a Christmas. You, like Mary, will deliver Christ into the world." (p. 91)

Where has Christ obviously "come out" in you? What are some areas where you see unmistakable evidence of spiritual transformation?

Read Galatians 5:19–26. What is Jesus saying to you there?

List the areas where you will begin trusting God for a deeper work, for Jesus to "show up" in your life.

REMINDERS

- Just as Jesus grew inside Mary, every Christian is indwelt by Christ.
- With God living inside us, we have a million resources we did not have before!
- God is less interested in your abilities and more interested in your willingness to trust him with everyday problems and opportunities.

13
A Cure for the Common Life

Ordinary Places

"Can we call the life of Christ 'common'? Nine-tenths of it we can. When you list the places Christ lived, draw a circle around the town named Nazareth—a single-camel map dot on the edge of boredom. For thirty of his thirty-three years, Jesus lived a common life. Aside from that one incident in the temple at the age of twelve, we have no record of what he said or did for the first thirty years he walked on this earth." (p. 96)

IMPRESSIONS

Get a highlighter and mark the sentences or phrases in chapter 13 of *Next Door Savior* that speak most forcefully to you. What about these statements moves you, or makes you stop and think hard about your own life? What's your overall impression to the content of this brief chapter?

What have been the three most amazing and exciting experiences of your life?

What stands out in your life as supremely "common," ordinary, routine? When do you most feel common and ordinary? Why?

What would your friends and family say are your most outstanding ("uncommon") qualities or abilities?

As you continue this study, pray this prayer (or one like it):

Lord, open my eyes. Help me to see you at work today in my life and in the world. And, please, Lord, open my ears. Enable me to hear the words you wish to whisper to my heart. Thank you for being my Savior, for coming to me, for being with me, for living in me. Amen.

GLIMPSES

Max notes the single statement from Mark's biography of Jesus that gives a glimpse into Christ's early adulthood years. It's a question asked by neighbors who, frankly, were surprised at Jesus' growing popularity: "Is not this the carpenter?" (Mark 6:3). That's all we have. Well, that, and one other barely noticeable comment from Luke: "When Jesus entered public life he was about thirty years old"(Luke 3:23 MSG).

These statements do not give enough for a detailed picture, but enough to speculate on an average day in the early life of Christ. Do that now. Use the space below to sketch out how a normal day might have unfolded in the life of Jesus when he was, say, twenty-four years old.

Read the last chapter in the book of Romans. What do you notice? What do you make of this long list of funny names? How many do you recognize? How many are household names? Who *were* these people? What does this tell you about the make-up of the early church? What does this suggest about your "average" life and the way God works in the world?

Ephesians 2:8–10 (NLT) makes some extraordinary claims to ordinary people:

God saved you by his special favor when you believed. And you can't take credit for this; it is a gift from God. Salvation is not a reward for the good things we have done, so none of us can boast about it. For we are God's masterpiece. He has created us anew in Christ Jesus, so that we can do the good things he planned for us long ago.

What did God do for us and why? What did he make us into? What are his plans and goals for us? Are they mundane or astonishing?

Encounters

"What a world he left." (p. 84)

What do you make of all the common, everyday references in the statements of Jesus?

What do these tell us?

Matthew 6:26–28 (references to birds and lilies)

Matthew 7:3 (a comment about sawdust)

Matthew 11:30 (a mention of a wooden yoke)

Matthew 13:31–32 (a few words about mustard seeds)

Matthew 16:2 (a statement regarding meteorology)

> "There is no event so commonplace but that God is present within it, always hiddenly, always leaving you room to recognize him or not recognize him. . . . See [your life] for the fathomless mystery that it is. In the boredom and pain of it no less than in the excitement and gladness: touch, taste, and smell your way to the holy and hidden heart of it because in the last analysis all moments are key moments, and life itself is grace."
>
> —FREDERICK BUECHNER, QUOTED IN *NEXT DOOR SAVIOR*

MUSINGS

Do you think Jesus was less holy all those years he spent in obscurity in Nazareth? Was God more pleased with him once he finally laid aside his carpentry tools and started teaching and healing? Why or why not?

If Jesus *never* sinned, and if it's true that he *always* pleased God (see John 8:29), what can we conclude about his unknown years from age 12 to age 30, during which he seemingly lived an average, common, everyday existence?

Martyred missionary Jim Elliot, subject of the best-selling book *Shadow of the Almighty*, once counseled, "Wherever you are, be all there." What do you think he meant? Why is this a wise warning for our impatient, time-wasting, thrill-seeking generation?

Encounters

"The places he went to reach us show how far he will go to touch us." (p. 86)

Someone has suggested that, if we're not careful, it is actually possible to "miss your life" in the same way that one can "miss a flight." If we spend too much time looking back with regret, or too many hours anxiously scanning the horizon to try to see what is coming next, we miss our lives—the amazing wonder and mystery of life—unfolding all around us.

How well do *you* savor your days, living fully in the moment? How often do you wish away your common life—waiting for the next big adventure?

The classic holiday movie *It's a Wonderful Life* (starring Jimmy Stewart and Donna Reed) tells the story of George Bailey, a common man in a small town who despairs of his "average" life. When he wishes he had never been born, his guardian angel lets him see how different (and how dismal) the world would have been had he not been around to touch the lives of so many neighbors and friends. The message? *Ordinary people can have an extraordinary impact.*

This is the Bible's message too! Love others. Serve. Do what is right *today*. Don't worry about being noticed by others. *God* is watching. Persevere in the little things and the hard times. Be faithful. It may not seem like a big deal at the time. But *over* time, our little acts of obedience and our long-term diligence will result in a huge impact.

DECISIONS

"You lead a common life. Punctuated by occasional weddings, job transfers, bowling trophies, and graduations—a few highlights—but mainly the day-to-day rhythm that you share with the majority of humanity. . . . You need to know how to succeed at being common. Commonhood has its perils, you know. A face in the crowd can feel lost in the crowd. You tend to think you are unproductive, wondering if you'll leave any lasting contribution." (p. 95)

Does this describe you? On a scale of 1-10 (with 1 = "My life seems like a cold bowl of tasteless oatmeal," and 10 = "My life feels like a sizzling platter of delicious, spicy fajitas!"), how would you rate your overall mood just now?

How does it encourage you to know that Jesus was extremely familiar with routine, with life in a ho-hum place, with relating to everyday situations and regular folks?

Encounters

_____
_____
_____
_____
_____
_____
_____
_____
_____
_____
_____
_____
_____
_____
_____
_____
_____

"The virgin birth is more, much more, than a Christmas story; it is a picture of how close Christ will come to you." (p. 90)

"Jesus listened to his common life. Are you listening to yours? Rain pattering against a window. Silent snow in April. The giggle of a baby on a crowded plane. Seeing a sunrise while the world sleeps. Are these not personal epistles? Can't God speak through a Monday commute or a midnight diaper change? Take notes on your life." (p. 97)

How could you begin to listen to your life more consistently—starting today?

Here are the facts:

- God created us—*in his image.*
- When we rebelled against God, ruining our lives, Christ left heaven to come find and rescue us.
- Then Jesus commissioned us to partner with him in a cosmic and eternal cause—building his church.

> "Let's follow the sandalprints. Let's sit on the cold, hard floor of the cave in which he was born. Let's smell the sawdust of the carpentry shop. Let's hear his sandals slap the hard trails of Galilee. Let's sigh as we touch the healed sores of the leper. Let's smile as we see his compassion with the woman at the well. Let's cringe as we hear the hissing of hell's Satan. . . . Let's try to see him."
> —GOD CAME NEAR

So, what are we to conclude? How does that change your view of who you are and why you're here?

REMINDERS

- Like us, Christ lived a mostly common life. He understands what it means to live and labor in apparent obscurity.
- Like Jesus, you have the chance to live an uncommon life. You can see every moment as sacred, every person as special, and every act—no matter how "small" or "mundane"—as an act of worship.

14
Oh, to Be DTP-Free!

Religious Places

"A computer virus is a common cold compared to the Chernobyl-level attack you and I must face. Think of your mind as a computer. . . . Think of your strengths as software. . . . We are different, but we each have a computer and software, and, sadly, we have viruses. You and I are infected by . . . mental viruses . . . known as anxiety, bitterness, anger, guilt, shame, greed, and insecurity. They worm their way into your system and diminish, even disable, your mind. We call these DTPs: destructive thought patterns." (pp. 103–104)

IMPRESSIONS

It won't take you more than a few minutes to read and/or review chapter 14 of *Next Door Savior*. While you're looking back at those pages, think about these questions:

What ideas here are new to me?
What does this chapter help me see that I need to *stop* doing?
What does this chapter show me that I need to *start* doing?

Take stock of your mind. On each of the following spectrums or scales, place an X close to where you think your own mental condition or habits currently are:

Depression	———————————	Joy
Anxiety	———————————	Peace
Confusion	———————————	Clarity
Frazzled	———————————	Focused

Scheming	————————————	Trusting
Impurity	————————————	Purity
Bitterness	————————————	Forgiveness
Self-absorbed	————————————	Other-focused
Doom/gloom	————————————	Hope
Stuff of earth	————————————	Eternal things

Explain the response(s) that most concern you (use the "Encounters" page that follows if you run out of space).

When you daydream, where does your mind like to wander?

Proverbs 23:7 announces that as a person "thinks in his heart, so *is* he" (NKJV). In other words, our beliefs determine our behavior. If that's true (and it is), our innermost thoughts and deepest convictions are the most important things about us. The most significant project in which we can ever engage, therefore, is making sure our beliefs line up with the truth of God's Word.

As you begin this time of reflection, ask God to open your eyes, to give you insight and clarity. Ask for divine help to discern exactly where and how your thoughts and beliefs need to change. Ask him to put you on the right path to a "renewed mind."

GLIMPSES

Consider what the Bible says about the human mind:

- "Although they knew God, they neither glorified him as God nor gave thanks to him, but their thinking became futile and their foolish hearts were darkened. Although they claimed to be wise, they became fools" (Romans 1:21–22 NIV).
- "[T]he ungodly . . . are hopelessly confused. Their closed minds are full of darkness; they are far away from the life of God because they have shut their minds and hardened their hearts against him. They don't care anymore about right and wrong, and they have given themselves over to immoral ways. Their lives are filled with all kinds of impurity and greed" (Ephesians 4:17–19 NLT).

Encounters

"Proliferating throughout Scripture is a preposition that leaves no doubt—the
preposition in. Jesus lives in his children." (p. 90)

- "Don't copy the behavior and customs of this world, but let God transform you into a new person by changing the way you think" (Romans 12:2 NLT).

How would you summarize the mental condition of the human race? According to the Scriptures, what needs to happen? What does God want to do in us?

Max labels our problem "DTPs" (destructive thought patterns). He compares these wrong, renegade beliefs to computer viruses that wreak havoc, and says: "Trace our mental viruses back to the fall of the first man, Adam. Because of sin, our minds are full of dark thoughts" (p. 104). The basic idea here is that until we begin thinking rightly, we will never act rightly.

What situations in your life can you think of where wrong beliefs led to wrong choices? (For example: "I thought for sure the stock market was going to take off, and so I sunk all my savings in a mutual fund. It went down 27 percent the next twelve months"; or "I thought fulfillment would come through business success, so I worked 80 hours a week. It ultimately cost me my marriage.")

Enter Jesus, our next door Savior. We don't get a glimpse of Christ's mind as a newborn infant, but we do have this anecdote from Luke's gospel:

Luke 2:41–49 (NLT)

Every year Jesus' parents went to Jerusalem for the Passover festival. When Jesus was twelve years old, they attended the festival as usual. After the celebration was over, they started home to Nazareth, but Jesus stayed behind in Jerusalem. His parents didn't miss him at first, because they assumed he was with friends among the other travelers. But when he didn't show up that evening, they started to look for him among their relatives and friends. When they couldn't find him, they went back to Jerusalem to search for him there. Three days later they finally discovered him. He was in the Temple, sitting among the religious teachers, discussing deep questions with them. And all who heard him were amazed at his understanding and his answers.

His parents didn't know what to think. "Son!" his mother said to him. "Why have you done this to us? Your father and I have been frantic, searching for you everywhere."

"But why did you need to search?" he asked. "You should have known that I would be in my Father's house."

Encounters

*"Christ grew in Mary until he had to come out.
Christ will grow in you until the same occurs." (p. 91)*

What do you make of this astonishing scene? What kind of window do you get into the mind of the pre-adolescent Christ?

"What made Jesus different? The Bible is silent about his IQ. When it comes to the RAM size of his mental computer, we are told nothing. But when it comes to his purity of mind, we are given this astounding claim: Christ "knew no sin" (2 Cor. 5:21). Peter says Jesus 'did not sin, neither was guile found in his mouth' (1 Peter 2:22 KJV). John lived next to him for three years and concluded, 'In Him there is no sin' (1 John 3:5). . . . Christ was followed by disciples, analyzed by crowds, criticized by family, and scrutinized by enemies, yet not one person would remember him committing even one sin." (pp. 105–106)

If Christ's behavior was flawless—not one sin, ever!—what can we conclude about his mind?

MUSINGS

"Lust wooed him. Greed lured him. Power called him. Jesus—the human—was tempted. But Jesus—the holy God—resisted. . . . The word sinless *has never survived cohabitation with another person. Those who knew Christ best, however, spoke of his purity in unison and with conviction. And because he was sinless, his mind was stainless. DTP-less. No wonder people were 'amazed at his teaching' (Mark 1:22 NCV). His mind was virus-free." (p. 106)*

Why does Christ's mental and moral perfection matter to us?

Max writes: "Remember the twelve-year-old boy in the temple? The one with sterling thoughts and a Teflon mind? Guess what? That is God's goal for you! You are made to be like Christ! God's priority is that you be 'transformed by the renewing of your mind' (Romans 12:2 NIV)". (p. 106)

If you could change three unlovely character qualities or habits, what would they be? Now, think *deeply* about these ingrained ways of living. What wrong thoughts or beliefs lurk in your soul that cause you to act in these ways?

Encounters

"God seems less interested in talent and more interested in trust." (p. 92)

> "You may have been born virus-prone, but you don't have to live that way. There is hope for your head! Are you a worrywart? Don't have to be one forever. Guilt plagued and shame stained? Prone to anger? Jealousy? God can take care of that. God can change your mind."
>
> —NEXT DOOR SAVIOR

Note: Life change is hard work. It's tough stuff. And to complicate matters, we have an enemy who wants to keep us blinded and in the dark. He doesn't want us to see the truth, much less be liberated by it. So he will fight you here. He will try to distract you with TV or chores. He will suggest you throw up your hands and say, "This is too confusing—how should *I* know why I do what I do! I'm not a psychiatrist. Hey, this is just the way I am!"

Don't buy Satan's lies. And don't give in to mental or moral laziness. We *have* to ponder and search and probe! As one man observed, "Thinking is hard work—which probably explains why so few people do it." We must take time, make time, for honest reflection. If we don't examine our hearts, we will never uncover the truth. Remember, it's the truth that sets us free—the truth about who we are (even when what we discover is painful or embarrassing)—And, more important, the truth about who God is and what he says and promises.

What does 2 Corinthians 3:18 say about the prospect of being transformed?

Max observes: "To behold him is to become like him. As Christ dominates your thoughts, he changes you from one degree of glory to another until—hang on!—you are ready to live with him (p. 107)."

Use your sanctified imagination. What do you suppose it will be like to have a renewed, glorified, "virus-free" mind in heaven?

DECISIONS

"Do you have any DTPs (destructive thought patterns)? When you see the successful, are you jealous? When you see the struggler, are you pompous? . . . Ever argue with someone in your mind? Rehash or rehearse your hurts? Do you assume the worst about the future?" (p. 104)

Encounters

"Do commoners rate in heaven? Does God love common people?" (p. 95)

Well, do you? Do *you* struggle with any of those temptations? How about with other DTPs?

Answer these questions that Max poses: "Suppose you could relive your life sans any guilt, lust, vengeance, insecurity, or fear. Never wasting mental energy on gossip or scheming. Would you be any different? What would you have that you don't have? What would you have done that you haven't done?" (p. 104).

In conclusion, let's get down to everyday practicalities. How does a person actually begin to change the way he or she thinks? Before you answer, read carefully these passages:

- "Let heaven fill your thoughts. Do not think only about things down here on earth" (Colossians 3:2 NLT).
- "The weapons we fight with are not the weapons of the world. On the contrary, they have divine power to demolish strongholds. We demolish arguments and every pretension that sets itself up against the knowledge of God, and we take captive every thought to make it obedient to Christ" (2 Corinthians 10:4–5 NIV).
- "Finally, beloved, whatever is true, whatever is honorable, whatever is just, whatever is pure, whatever is pleasing, whatever is commendable, if there is any excellence and if there is anything worthy of praise, think about these things" (Philippians 4:8 NRSV).

What do those truths/commands look like (practically speaking) when we apply them to our daily lives? How would you explain this "renewing your mind" concept to a young, struggling friend?

Compose a prayer that expresses your desire to embark on a course to deeply change the way you think.

Encounters

_"If the word common describes you, take heart—
you're in fine company. It also describes Christ."_ (p. 96)

REMINDERS

- What we *think* dictates how we *live*.

- We desperately need to "change our minds," . . . otherwise we will never see our lives changed.

- Jesus, our next door Savior, has a perfect, sin-free mind, and he is in the process of making our minds just like his.

- We are called to actively participate with Christ in "renewing our minds" (Romans 12:2).

15
Tire Kicker to Car Buyer

Unexpected Places

"A baptismal ceremony is an odd place to find the Son of God. He should be the baptizer not the baptizee. Why would Christ want to be baptized? If baptism was, and is, for the confessed sinner, how do we explain the immersion of history's only sinless soul?" (p. 112)

IMPRESSIONS

Chapter 15 of *Next Door Savior* is only three pages long! (Don't you wish some of those "classics" you were forced to read back in high school literature class could have been so concise!) Take a couple of minutes to look back over the content.

What stands out to you? What's the big idea of this chapter? What "aha!" moments or thoughts that you've never had before did it prompt?

In what clubs or organizations are you active? What's involved in becoming a member of each? What rituals or physical objects demonstrate your association with these groups?

What church traditions do you enjoy the most and why? Which ones do you find the most curious or tiresome? Why, do you think?

Before beginning this lesson, pray this wonderful old Celtic prayer:

Lord of my heart, give me vision to inspire me, that, working or resting, I may always think of you.

Lord of my heart, give me light to guide me, that, at home or abroad, I may always walk in your way.

Lord of my heart, give me wisdom to direct me, that, thinking or acting, I may always discern right from wrong . . .

Heart of my own heart, whatever befall me, rule over my thoughts and feelings, my words and action.

(Quoted in *Between Heaven and Earth*, by Ken Gire [San Francisco: HarperCollins, 1997], p. 138)

GLIMPSES

In the third chapter of Matthew's Gospel, we find Jesus popping up in an unexpected place, doing something very unexpected. Here's the story:

> Then Jesus went from Galilee to the Jordan River to be baptized by John. But John didn't want to baptize him. "I am the one who needs to be baptized by you," he said, "so why are you coming to me?" But Jesus said, "It must be done, because we must do everything that is right." So then John baptized him. After his baptism, as Jesus came up out of the water, the heavens were opened and he saw the Spirit of God descending like a dove and settling on him. And a voice from heaven said, "This is my beloved Son, and I am fully pleased with him." (Matthew 3:13–17 NLT)

Why was John reluctant to baptize Jesus?

Max points out that Matthew 3:15 in the Contemporary English Version reads: "Jesus answered, 'For now this is how it should be, because *we* must do all that God wants *us* to do'" (emphasis mine). What is significant about the pronouns Jesus uses in this verse?

What is heaven's response to this event in the life of Christ? What do you see here that surprises you?

Encounters

_____

_____

_____

_____

_____

_____

_____

_____

_____

_____

_____

_____

_____

_____

_____

_____

_____

_____

"Next time your life feels ordinary, take your cue from Christ. Pay attention to your work and your world." (p. 97)

What do the following Bible passages reveal about baptism and about Jesus? What does the act of baptism signify?

- "[We] became part of Christ when we were baptized" (Romans 6:3 NCV).
- "For all of you who were baptized into Christ have clothed yourselves with Christ" (Galatians 3:27 NIV).
- "There is now no condemnation for those who are in Christ Jesus" (Romans 8:1 NIV).

MUSINGS

Midway through chapter 15, Max tells of an incident in which his daughter Sara ignored a "Do Not Touch" sign and accidentally broke some merchandise in an airport gift shop (see page 112). How did Max respond? How is his response a good picture of what our heavenly Father has done for us?

What is the purpose of the ritual of baptism? How do you know?

How is a person forgiven and made right with God?

> "What do you do with a man who claims to be God, yet hates religion? What do you do with a man who calls himself the Savior, yet condemns systems? What do you do with a man who knows the place and time of his death, yet goes there anyway?"
>
> —AND THE ANGELS WERE SILENT

Max tells how, as a youngster in Texas, he used to go to a local drive-in on Friday nights with as many as twelve people crammed in the car, and he would point to the driver, telling the ticket seller, "We're with him." He concludes: "God doesn't tell you to climb into Christ's car; he tells you to climb into Christ! . . . He is your vehicle! Baptism celebrates your decision to take a seat. . . . We are not saved by the act, but the act demonstrates the way we are saved. We are given credit for a perfect life we did not lead—indeed, a life we could never lead" (p. 113).

Encounters

"*Jesus left Nazareth . . . and brought us to life. Perhaps we aren't so common after all.*" (p. 99)

How does this definition compare to what you were brought up to believe? Does this seem fair to you? Generous to you?

DECISIONS

"What do we owe? We owe God a perfect life. Perfect obedience to every command. Not just the command of baptism, but the commands of humility, honesty, integrity. We can't deliver, . . . but Christ can and he did. His plunge into the Jordan is a picture of his plunge into our sin. His baptism announces, "Let me pay." Your baptism responds, 'You bet I will.' He publicly offers. We publicly accept." (pp. 112–113)

When were you baptized? What does baptism mean to you?

If you have never been baptized, what is keeping you from participating in this meaningful testimony to identify with Christ and his people?

Think of three specific ways that you could show gratitude to Jesus Christ today for what he has done for you. Write them down—and do them!

REMINDERS

- Christ was baptized to demonstrate his willingness to identify fully with us.
- Baptism is meant to convey union or close association.
- Baptism doesn't save us; it signifies that we are identifying with Christ and his people.

16
The Long, Lonely Winter

Wilderness Places

"Parched promises. Sharp words. Shifting commitments. Burning anger. Rejections that cut. Miraging hope. Distant solutions ever beyond reach. This is the wilderness of the soul." (p. 117)

IMPRESSIONS

Chapter 16 of *Next Door Savior* talks about dry, rugged, wilderness places—both literal and spiritual. It asks the question, "Does Jesus have anything to say *to* us, any example *for* us when we go through life's hard times?" Read it (if you haven't already). Review it (if it's been a while since you pondered the content).

What strikes you? What, in the chapter, jars you or challenges your thinking? What gives you comfort or makes you uncomfortable? Try to put your thoughts into words in the space below.

Are you more of an indoor/big city person or an outdoor/country person? Why do you think that's the case?

Are you more into noise, activity, and crowds or into solitude and silence? How come?

Have you ever been in a real wilderness setting? To an actual desert? What was it like? Describe your experience. If not, what's the most remote place you've ever been?

This lesson delves into some hard and mysterious realities: suffering, temptation, weakness, and God's (often difficult) plans for our lives. A lot is at stake. If you wrestle with and somehow manage to grasp—even just partially—the truths here, you will be healthier and better equipped for whatever life throws at you. If, however, you choose to just skim superficially over the content, you will miss a prime opportunity for insight and growth.

Take a few moments to tell God what you need from him—not what your flesh wants, but what your heart deeply needs.

GLIMPSES

Immediately after Jesus' baptism (see the previous lesson), the earthly journey of our next door Savior takes a diabolical turn. Here's the story—an incident that contains important insights for us.

Luke 4:1-13 (NCV)

Jesus, filled with the Holy Spirit, returned from the Jordan River. The Spirit led Jesus into the desert where the devil tempted Jesus for forty days. Jesus ate nothing during that time, and when those days were ended, he was very hungry.

The devil said to Jesus, "If you are the Son of God, tell this rock to become bread."

Jesus answered, "It is written in the Scriptures: 'A person does not live by eating only bread.'"

Then the devil took Jesus and showed him all the kingdoms of the world in an instant. The devil said to Jesus, "I will give you all these kingdoms and all their power and glory. It has all been given to me, and I can give it to anyone I wish. If you worship me, then it will all be yours."

Jesus answered, "It is written in the Scriptures: 'You must worship the Lord your God and serve only him.'"

Then the devil led Jesus to Jerusalem and put him on a high place of the Temple. He said to Jesus, "If you are the Son of God, jump down. It is written in the Scriptures: 'He has put his angels in charge of you to watch over you.' It is also written: 'They will catch you in their hands so that you will not hit your foot on a rock.'"

Jesus answered, "But it also says in the Scriptures: 'Do not test the Lord your God.'"

After the devil had tempted Jesus in every way, he left him to wait until a better time.

What was the nature and number of Christ's temptations? Why those things? Why not some other kinds of enticement?

Encounters

"You and I are infected by destructive thoughts." (p. 104)

Max writes: "One more symptom of the badlands: You think the unthinkable. Jesus did. Wild possibilities crossed his mind. Teaming up with Satan? Opting to be a dictator and not a Savior? Torching Earth and starting over on Pluto? We don't know what he thought. We just know this. He was tempted. . . . The wilderness weakens resolve" (p. 118).

Do you agree? Do you think Jesus, even if only for a few fleeting moments, at least *thought* the unthinkable?

What does Luke 4:13 (NCV) indicate about the devil's schemes and his attack strategy? What do you think the phrase "a better time" means? *Better* for whom?

How does this incident parallel what we are told in James 4:7–8?

How did Jesus end up fighting the temptations of the evil one? What weapon(s) did he use?

MUSINGS

Don't miss the sequence of events. Jesus undergoes a glorious baptism experience in which he hears God the Father say, "You are my delight, and I am so proud of you. I love you beyond words!" Yet in the very next scene, God directs his beloved son into the harshest experience of his life (at least thus far).

What does this say to you about trials and God's love? Are you the type of person who equates comfort and ease with God's favor and hard times as evidence of God's disapproval? Why? Is this what the Bible teaches?

Is it a sin to be tempted? How do you know? On what do you base your answer?

Encounters

"God . . . changes the man by changing the mind." (p. 107)

If it is *not* wrong to be the target of the enemy's temptations, when *do* we cross the line into sin?

"You and I are no match for Satan. Jesus knows this. So he donned our jersey. Better still, he put on our flesh. He was 'tempted in every way, just as we are—yet was without sin' (Hebrews 4:15 NIV). And because he did, we pass with flying colors.

"God gives you Jesus' wilderness grade. Believe that. If you don't, the desert days will give you a one-two punch. The right hook is the struggle. The left jab is the shame for not prevailing against it. Trust his work.

"And trust his Word. Don't trust your emotions. Don't trust your opinions. Don't even trust your friends. In the wilderness heed only the voice of God."

—NEXT DOOR SAVIOR

Max challenges us with these words of warning: "You needn't journey to Israel to experience the wilderness. A cemetery will do just fine. So will a hospital. Grief can lead you into the desert. So can divorce or debt or depression. . . . Been through any transitions lately? A transfer? Job promotion? Job demotion? A new house? If so, be wary. The wilderness might be near" (pp. 117–118).

Well, what about it? Tragedies and transitions *do* lead to stress. And stress, if mismanaged, often becomes our weak excuse for getting in trouble. What about Max's questions above? What transitions are you facing these days?

"Binge-eating, budget-busting gambling, excessive drinking, pornography—all short-term solutions to deep-seated problems. Typically they have no appeal, but in the wilderness you give thought to the unthinkable" (p. 118). When have you seen this principle at work in your life? Perhaps during times of loneliness, emptiness, frustration, or boredom you have made some wrong, inappropriate choices. What happened?

Encounters

"Heaven will be wonderful, not because the streets are gold,
but because our thoughts will be pure." (p. 107)

DECISIONS

"The Second Adam has come to succeed where the first Adam failed. Jesus, however, faces a test far more severe. Adam was tested in a garden; Christ is in a stark wasteland. Adam faced Satan on a full stomach; Christ is in the midst of a fast. Adam had a companion: Eve. Christ has no one. Adam was challenged to remain sinless in a sinless world. Christ, on the other hand, is challenged to remain sinless in a sin-ridden world." (p. 119)

When have you been through a time of wilderness of the soul? What was that experience like? If you are in a dark, hard, tempting time right now, how are you faring? What is your strategy for not just surviving but thriving in such a time?

Max mentions Jesus' famous reply to Satan: "Man shall not live on bread alone, but on every word that proceeds out of the mouth of God" (Matthew 4:4—a quotation of Deuteronomy 8:3). He notes that the verb *proceeds* means, literally, "pouring out" (p. 121). In other words, the idea being conveyed is that God is *continually* speaking—*volumes* of truth—to anyone and everyone who will listen.

What do you think God is trying to say to *you* today, through this study?

To whom (spiritual friends, mentors, elders, church staff members, and others) can you turn for help?

How can a small group of fellow believers be a godsend in life's difficult moments? Are you in such a group now? If not, why not? If so, how can your group give you the support and encouragement you need today to keep going?

Encounters

_____

_____

_____

_____

_____

_____

_____

_____

_____

_____

_____

_____

_____

_____

_____

_____

_____

_____

_____

_____

*"So what are you waiting on? Apply God's antivirus. . . . Give him your best thoughts,
and see if he doesn't change your mind." (p. 107)*

"Jesus' weapon of choice was Scripture. . . . Everything you and I need for desert survival is in the Book. We simply need to heed it" (p. 120). What are your Bible reading and heeding habits? What is your plan for getting God's Word in your heart so that you might not sin against him (Psalm 119:11)?

REMINDERS

- We all face wilderness places in this life.
- Jesus has been there—he knows what we're up against. He can and does sympathize.
- Jesus passed his wilderness test with flying colors; he defeated our great enemy, the devil!
- Jesus is not only our Savior in times of trouble; he is our example.
- When we find ourselves in hard places, we must live by what God says, not by how we feel.

17
God Gets Into Things

Stormy Places

"When the ambulance takes our child or the disease takes our friend; when the economy takes our retirement or the two-timer takes our heart—can we . . . find Christ in the crisis?" (p. 125)

IMPRESSIONS

Chapter 17 wades into the age-old question: Where is God when life gets ugly? This is *not* an academic question; it gets to the core of human experience. It rubs up against the greatest mysteries of life: If God is all-good and all-wise and all-powerful, then how do we explain the stark fact of suffering and evil? Go back and look over the chapter, or read it now for the first time.

What sentences and paragraphs make the most sense to you and provide the most comfort? How did you feel as you were reading? What shocked, baffled, or angered you?

What has been the biggest crisis of your life? How did you make it through? What kept you going?

What would you say to the person who lost a loved one in New York, Washington, or Pennsylvania on September 11, 2001, if he or she asked you, "Where was God in the middle of this horror?"

Take a few minutes to ponder the following prayer by Dietrich Bonhoeffer. A German pastor, author, and theologian, Bonhoeffer composed these desperate words of trust while in a Nazi concentration camp on Christmas Day, 1943:

> I am lonely, but Thou leavest me not. I am feeble in heart, but Thou leavest me not. I am restless, but with Thee there is peace. . . . Thou knowest all man's distress. Thou abidest with me when all others have deserted me; Thou will not forget me, Thou seekest me. . . . Lord, whatsoever this day may bring, Thy name be praised. Be gracious unto me and help me. Grant me strength to bear whatsoever Thou dost send, And let not fear overrule me. I trust Thy grace, and commit my life wholly into Thy Hands. Whether I live or whether I die, I am with Thee and Thou art with me. O my Lord and my God. (Quoted in Ken Gire's *Between Heaven and Earth* [San Francisco: HarperCollins, 1997], pp. 253–254).

GLIMPSES

Perhaps in answer to humanity's common question, "Where was God when _____?" we have been given this historical record from Matthew 14:22–33 (NLT).

> Immediately after this, Jesus made his disciples get back into the boat and cross to the other side of the lake while he sent the people home. Afterward he went up into the hills by himself to pray. Night fell while he was there alone. Meanwhile, the disciples were in trouble far away from land, for a strong wind had risen, and they were fighting heavy waves. About three o'clock in the morning Jesus came to them, walking on the water. When the disciples saw him, they screamed in terror, thinking he was a ghost. But Jesus spoke to them at once. "It's all right," he said. "I am here! Don't be afraid." Then Peter called to him, "Lord, if it's really you, tell me to come to you by walking on water."
>
> "All right, come," Jesus said. So Peter went over the side of the boat and walked on the water toward Jesus. But when he looked around at the high waves, he was terrified and began to sink. "Save me, Lord!" he shouted.
>
> Instantly Jesus reached out his hand and grabbed him. "You don't have much faith," Jesus said. "Why did you doubt me?"
>
> And when they climbed back into the boat, the wind stopped. Then the disciples worshiped him. "You really are the Son of God!" they exclaimed.

According to the first part of this passage, what were the disciples' activities, thoughts, and feelings? How long did this weather crisis last?

Encounters

_____

_____

_____

_____

_____

_____

_____

_____

_____

_____

_____

_____

_____

_____

_____

_____

"A baptismal ceremony is an odd place to find the Son of God." (p. 112)

What about Jesus? What part does he play in the disciples' predicament? *Where* is Jesus, and what is he doing as this fierce storm begins to howl? (NOTE: Read the report of this incident found in Mark 6:45–52 and note especially verse 48.) Does this comfort you or concern you as you ponder your own storms of life?

Max notes that a literal translation of Christ's announcement in Matthew 14:27 would be "Courage! I am! Don't be afraid." He adds: "Translators tinker with his words for obvious reasons. 'I am' sounds truncated. 'I am here' or 'It is I' feels more complete. But what Jesus shouted in the storm was simply the magisterial 'I am'" (p. 126).

Look up these two verses, consider the context of each, and note the wording in each place:

- Exodus 3:14

- John 8:58

> "Hope is not a granted wish or a favor performed; no, it is far greater than that. It is a zany, unpredictable dependence on a God who loves to surprise us out of our socks."
>
> —GOD CAME NEAR

What is the significance of Christ using the words "I am" to describe himself?

MUSINGS

The story of the disciples in the storm has what every reasonable person would call a happy ending. Jesus shows up in the nick of time and makes everything okay. But not all stories end like that. Just pick up a newspaper or catch the news on cable tonight. *Lots* of times boats sink and people drown. Instead of awe-filled worship services (see Matthew 14:33), people find themselves at grief-filled funeral services.

What are we to make of this? How do you respond?

Encounters

*"If baptism was, and is, for the confessed sinner,
how do we explain the immersion of history's only sinless soul?" (p. 112)*

How can the hope of heaven, and the promise of Revelation 21 and 22, give us the perspective we need?

In the worst times of your life, has God seemed near and real to you or distant and hidden?

Max writes: "Prone to be people of the past tense, we reminisce. Not God. Unwavering in strength, he need never say, 'I was.' . . . He does not change. He is the 'I am' God. 'Jesus Christ is the same yesterday, today, and forever' (Heb. 13:8, NLT)". (p. 127) How does it bolster your faith to know that God is unchanging? In what ways is God's eternal sameness a comfort to you in a world that is in constant upheaval?

Max concludes the chapter with the story of a woman lost in a bad part of New York who prayed for a sign of God's presence and then was comforted by a harmonica-playing homeless man. How? He started playing her mom's favorite hymn.

Lots of folks call situations like that mere coincidences. A few would shake their heads and accuse the lady of wishful thinking. What do *you* call it? Can you think of a rough time in your life when circumstances convinced you that God was with you and looking out for you?

DECISIONS

"From the center of the storm, the unwavering Jesus shouts, 'I am.' Tall in the Trade Tower wreckage. Bold against the Galilean waves. ICU, battlefield, boardroom, prison cell, or maternity ward—whatever your storm, 'I am.'" (p. 127)

Suppose you are discussing this passage and these ideas with a friend when he or she says, "Look. It's easy to talk about Jesus being with the disciples in the storm. When all was said and done, the storm died down and everyone's life was spared. Try telling my brother who lost his wife and both daughters in a head-on collision with a drunk driver that Jesus was with *them*! I'm sorry, but that just isn't a lot of comfort." What would you say?

Encounters

"Since you and I cannot pay, Christ did." (p. 112)

Who do you know who is in a storm right now? How can you be a help and a comfort today?

What difference do Matthew 28:20 and Hebrews 13:5 make when you are feeling as though God is absent from your life?

What is the single most important message you sense God saying to you in this time of study and reflection?

REMINDERS

- God often *seems* absent when we are going through the storms of life.
- The truth is that Jesus is the great "I am." Our next door Savior is always with us.

18
Hope or Hype?

The Highest Place

"The definitive voice in the universe is Jesus. He is not one among many voices; he is the One Voice over all voices." (p. 134)

IMPRESSIONS

In fifty words or less, how would you summarize chapter 18 of this book? What's the main message?

As you reflect on all the Bible passages you've pondered and all the insights into Christ you've gained so far in your reading of *Next Door Savior* and working through the guidebook, what truths stand out above the rest?

What have been the most significant lessons you've learned? What would you say is the biggest change in your life as a result of this study?

Our world—as Max points out—is very much like a carnival midway (p. 131). Especially when it comes to spirituality and philosophy. Lots of people believe (and are quick to *spout*) lots of different ideas—some of them quite bizarre. The result is a confusing cacophony of conflicting voices, and, at the end of the day, countless disillusioned people.

What belief systems or religions do you know the most about? Least about? What aberrant spiritual views are gaining popularity in your city or region? How is Christianity unique among the religions of the world?

With what you know of Jesus Christ and the claims of the gospel, why would anyone look anywhere else for salvation and help and hope? To what do you attribute the popularity of fringe groups and cults?

Use the apostle Paul's prayer for some young believers (adapted from Colossians 1:9–11 NLT) as a model for your own prayer as you begin this study:

God, please give me a complete understanding of what you want me to do in my life. Make me wise with spiritual wisdom. Then the way I live will always honor and please you, and I will continually do good, kind things for others. All the while, I will learn to know you better and better. Strengthen me with your glorious power so that I will have all the patience and endurance I need. Fill me with joy. In Christ's name I pray. Amen.

GLIMPSES

For this particular study on the uniqueness and supremacy of Christ, we go to a mountaintop of Israel and we witness a spectacular event. Here is Luke 9:28–36, from the Contemporary English Version of the Bible:

About eight days later Jesus took Peter, John, and James with him and went up on a mountain to pray. While he was praying, his face changed, and his clothes became shining white. Suddenly Moses and Elijah were there speaking with him. They appeared in heavenly glory and talked about all that Jesus' death in Jerusalem would mean. Peter and the other two disciples had been sound asleep. All at once they woke up and saw how glorious Jesus was. They also saw the two men who were with him. Moses and Elijah were about to leave, when Peter said to Jesus, "Master, it is good for us to be here! Let us make three shelters, one for you, one for Moses, and one for Elijah." But Peter did not know what he was talking about.

While Peter was still speaking, a shadow from a cloud passed over them, and they were frightened as the cloud covered them. From the cloud a voice spoke, "This is my chosen Son. Listen to what he says!" After the voice had spoken, Peter, John, and James saw only Jesus. For some time they kept quiet and did not say anything about what they had seen.

What's going on here? Describe the change in Jesus.

Encounters

_____

_____

_____

_____

_____

_____

_____

_____

_____

_____

_____

_____

_____

_____

_____

_____

"His plunge into the Jordan is a picture of his plunge into our sin. His baptism announces, 'Let me pay.'" (p. 113)

Why Moses and Elijah? Why not Abraham and David? Do you agree with Max that perhaps their purpose was to comfort Jesus? Why or why not?

> "Many people recoil at such a distinction. Call Jesus godly, godlike, God inspired. Call him 'a voice' but not 'the voice'; a good man but not God-man. But *good man* is precisely the terminology we cannot use. A good man would not say what he said or claim what he claimed. A liar would. Or a God would. Call him anything in between, and you have a dilemma. No one believed that Jesus was equal with God more than Jesus did."
>
> —NEXT DOOR SAVIOR

What happened when Peter interrupted the proceedings with his ideas about erecting tents or building monuments? How did God single out Jesus as the one worthy of ultimate attention and honor and glory?

Consider what the apostle Paul wrote about the supremacy of Christ:

"Christ is the one through whom God created everything in heaven and earth. He made the things we can see and the things we can't see—kings, kingdoms, rulers, and authorities. Everything has been created through him and for him. He existed before everything else began, and he holds all creation together. Christ is the head of the church, which is his body. He is the first of all who will rise from the dead, so he is first in everything. For God in all his fullness was pleased to live in Christ, and by him God reconciled everything to himself. He made peace with everything in heaven and on earth by means of his blood on the cross" (Colossians 1:16–20 NLT).

How does this description elevate Christ over everything and everyone else? In what way is Christ special and unique?

MUSINGS

Conventional "wisdom" says: "There is no such thing as absolute truth—it doesn't really matter *what* you believe, as long as you're sincere." What is the logical problem with this argument?

Encounters

"You can often chalk up wilderness wanderings to transition." (p. 118)

Imagine the outcome if scientists operated by such a philosophy in the laboratory. Or if airline mechanics, bridge engineers, and surgeons embraced a "whatever—anything goes—everything is acceptable" approach in their jobs. In what everyday situations, if you followed that kind of sloppy reasoning, would you end up in *big* trouble?

Why, when we come to the realm of spirituality, do we seem to think that every opinion has equal worth?

"The Torah sends you to Moses. The Koran sends you to Muhammad. Buddhists invite you to meditate; spiritists, to levitate. A palm reader wants your hand. The TV evangelist wants your money. One neighbor consults her stars. Another reads the cards. The agnostic believes no one can know. The hedonist doesn't care to know. Atheists believe there is nothing to know. . . . What do you do? Where's a person to go? Mecca? Salt Lake City? Rome? Therapy? Aromatherapy?" (pp. 131–132).

Where and when did you first realize that Christ is unique? What happened?

Why can't Jesus simply be labeled a good man or a great moral teacher? How do his clear claims to be God eliminate those possibilities?

Do you see why—if Jesus really *is* God in the flesh—the Christian faith has to be viewed as the ultimate explanation of reality, and all the other major religions of the world must be wrong?

Encounters

"What was unimaginable prior to the wilderness becomes possible in it." (p. 118)

> "The apostles sparked a movement. The people became followers of the death-conqueror. They couldn't hear enough or say enough about him. People began to call them 'Christians.' Christ was their model, their message. They preached 'Jesus Christ and him crucified,' not for the lack of another topic but because they couldn't exhaust this one."
>
> —SIX HOURS ONE FRIDAY

DECISIONS

"Call him crazy, or crown him as king. Dismiss him as a fraud, or declare him to be God. Walk away from him, or bow before him, but don't play games with him. Don't call him a great man. Don't list him among decent folk. Don't clump him with Moses, Elijah, Buddha, Joseph Smith, Muhammad, or Confucius. He didn't leave that option. He is either God or godless. Heaven sent or hell born. All hope or all hype. But nothing in between." (p. 135)

Are you crystal clear on who Jesus is? Are you sure you are God's child and that you have eternal life? On what do you base your beliefs?

A neighbor accuses you of being "narrow-minded" and "intolerant." He calls you a "religious bigot" for insisting that Jesus is the only way to God. (Actually, all you did was quote Christ himself—specifically, his words from John 14:6.) How would you defend yourself?

Can we "argue people into God's kingdom"? Should we even try? (Hint: See 1 Peter 3:15.)

Apologetics is a branch of theology devoted to defending the claims of Christianity. The goal is to show that our faith is rooted in history and based on sound facts and reasons. Have you ever taken a course or read a book that explains *what* you believe and *why*? What are your biggest unanswered questions about God or the Christian faith?

Encounters

"The wilderness is the maternity ward for addictions." (p. 118)

How do you think differently and feel differently after this time of study of reflection? How do you intend to act differently (be specific)?

REMINDERS

- Jesus Christ is absolutely unique in the universe.
- Jesus claimed to be divine, and he did not discourage his followers from worshiping him.
- Every person must make a decision about who Jesus is.
- As Almighty God in human form, Christ is worthy of our undivided attention.

19
Abandoned!

Godforsaken Places

" *'My God, my God, why did you abandon me?' Why did Christ scream those words? So you'll never have to.*" *(p. 142)*

IMPRESSIONS

As we near the end of this *Next Door Savior Guidebook*, we are moving through the final days of Christ's earthly life and ministry. Chapter 19 of the book takes us to a grim hill outside Jerusalem, a bloody place nicknamed "the Skull." There we will be forced to stomach some gruesome sights. There we will have to wrestle with some of the most mind-boggling words Jesus ever spoke.

What's your overall take on this chapter—on the actual Bible events described and on the description itself?

What did you *think* as you were reading? What did you *feel*? What, if anything, did you *decide*? Take a few moments to review, reflect, and record your impressions.

Probably in your life you've seen at least one movie depiction of Christ's crucifixion. Perhaps you've even seen a live Passion Play or Easter presentation with Jesus on the cross. How did (or how do) such things affect you?

Describe a time when you felt far away from God. Perhaps you were wrestling with guilt or loneliness or dealing with a tremendous trial. Would you say you felt *abandoned*, left to go it alone? Jot down some phrases and feelings that describe that dark time.

When is the last time you did something extremely difficult and terribly scary—something you truly did NOT want to do? Why did you do it? What happened in the end?

Before you begin this portion of the guidebook, spend a few minutes meditating on Psalm 88 (NLT), an honest prayer expressing feelings of abandonment.

O LORD, God of my salvation, I have cried out to you day and night. Now hear my prayer; listen to my cry. For my life is full of troubles, and death draws near. I have been dismissed as one who is dead, like a strong man with no strength left. They have abandoned me to death, and I am as good as dead. I am forgotten, cut off from your care. You have thrust me down to the lowest pit, into the darkest depths. Your anger lies heavy on me; wave after wave engulfs me.

You have caused my friends to loathe me; you have sent them all away. I am in a trap with no way of escape. My eyes are blinded by my tears. Each day I beg for your help, O LORD; I lift my pleading hands to you for mercy. Of what use to the dead are your miracles? Do the dead get up and praise you?

Can those in the grave declare your unfailing love? In the place of destruction, can they proclaim your faithfulness? Can the darkness speak of your miracles? Can anyone in the land of forgetfulness talk about your righteousness?

O LORD, I cry out to you. I will keep on pleading day by day. O LORD, why do you reject me? Why do you turn your face away from me? I have been sickly and close to death since my youth. I stand helpless and desperate before your terrors. Your fierce anger has overwhelmed me. Your terrors have cut me off. They swirl around me like floodwaters all day long. They have encircled me completely. You have taken away my companions and loved ones; only darkness remains.

GLIMPSES

The shocking betrayal has taken place. "Loyal" friends have fled like a pack of scalded dogs. And from that point, the evil just snowballs—bold-faced lies in a kangaroo court. Sick mockings

Encounters

"Doubt your doubts before you doubt your beliefs." (p. 121)

followed by savage beatings. And at last the ultimate cruelty—a bloodied rag doll of a man skewered onto a Roman cross. We pick up the story in Matthew 27:45–46 (TEV):

> At noon the whole country was covered with darkness, which lasted for three hours. At about three o'clock Jesus cried out with a loud shout, "Eli, Eli, lema sabachthani?" which means, "My God, my God, why did you abandon me?"

How do you explain this thick darkness? What do you think of the cryptic description of that moment by the historian Dionysius: "Either the God of nature is suffering, or the machine of the world is tumbling into ruin"? (p. 140).

Max observes: "As Jesus looks for God, can he find him? No. Forsaken. Wait a second. Doesn't David tell us, 'I have never seen the righteous forsaken' (Psalm 37:25 NIV)? Did David misspeak? Did Jesus misstep? Neither. In this hour Jesus is anything but righteous. But his mistakes aren't his own. 'Christ carried our sins in his body on the cross so we would stop living for sin and start living for what is right' (1 Pet. 2:24 NCV)" (p. 141).

What are the consequences—both personal and universal, both immediate and long-term, both bad and good—of Christ's agonizing experience on the cross?

Max writes: "As the Romans lifted the cross, they unwittingly placed Christ in the very position in which he came to die—between man and God. A priest on his own altar" (p. 140). These words remind us of a passage that explains Jesus' actions, his willingness to go to the cross:

> So Christ has now become the High Priest over all the good things that have come. He has entered that great, perfect sanctuary in heaven, not made by human hands and not part of this created world. Once for all time he took blood into that Most Holy Place, but not the blood of goats and calves. He took his own blood, and with it he secured our salvation forever. Under the old system, the blood of goats and bulls and the ashes of a young cow could cleanse people's bodies from ritual defilement. Just think how much more the blood of Christ will purify our hearts from deeds that lead to death so that we can worship the living God. For by the power of the eternal Spirit, Christ offered himself to God as a perfect sacrifice for our sins. (Hebrews 9:11–14 NLT)

Encounters

_____
_____
_____
_____
_____
_____
_____
_____
_____
_____
_____
_____
_____
_____
_____
_____
_____
_____

"The presence of troubles doesn't surprise us.
The absence of God, however, undoes us." (p. 125)

What insight does this passage shed on Christ's work on our behalf?

Now, do you see how that awful day at Golgotha could come to be labeled "Good Friday"?

MUSINGS

"In an act that broke the heart of the Father, yet honored the holiness of heaven, sin-purging judgment flowed over the sinless Son of the ages." (p. 142)

Why did Christ have to die? Or, put it this way: What would have happened if he had never made a perfect sacrifice for sin?

Of the various kinds of pain that Christ endured on the cross, which do you think was probably the most piercing and why?

- Physical—the cruelty of crucifixion
- Mental/Emotional—the indignity and loneliness of it all, the jeers of the crowd, and so forth
- Spiritual—becoming sin, bearing the judgment of the world

A few of Christ's followers lingered at the foot of the cross—weeping. Many stood at a safe distance (Peter even denied knowing Jesus). Why the difference? Had you been alive at the time and one of his disciples, which group do you suspect you might have been a part of?

The desperate words spoken by Christ from the cross, "My God, my God, why did you abandon me?" are actually found in Psalm 22:1 (TEV). Jesus was quoting David. Read that entire psalm. What is the significance of this repetition?

Encounters

"We can deal with the ambulance if God is in it. We can stomach the ICU if God is in it. We can face the empty house if God is in it. Is he?" (p. 126)

There are countless theories about why the sky turned black as Jesus was being crucified. What's your best guess as to what was going on there? (Hint: See Amos 8:9–10.)

> "To the casual observer the six hours are mundane, . . . but to the handful of awestruck witnesses the most maddening of miracles is occurring. God is on a cross. The creator of the universe is being executed. . . . And there is no one to save him, for he is sacrificing himself."
>
> —SIX HOURS
> ONE FRIDAY

DECISIONS

Max concludes chapter 19 with these words: "See Christ on the cross? That's a gossiper hanging there. See Jesus? Embezzler. Liar. Bigot. See the crucified carpenter? He's a wife beater. Porn addict and murderer. See Bethlehem's boy? Call him by his other names—Adolf Hitler, Osama bin Laden, and Jeffrey Dahmer. . . . With hands nailed open, he invited God, 'Treat me as you would treat them!' And God did. In an act that broke the heart of the Father, yet honored the holiness of heaven, sin-purging judgment flowed over the sinless Son of the ages" (p. 142).

How does it make you feel to see Christ linked with history's most evil men and associated with evil acts?

In 1 Peter 2:24, a verse we looked at earlier, we read that Christ carried all our sins in his body. What does this mean to you today?

A lot of unchurched people avoid God and steer clear of conversations about Jesus because they think God is out to get them or make their lives miserable. Is that the message you've been getting from the Bible passages highlighted in *Next Door Savior*? How would these reminders of God's infinite love (and *especially* the vivid truth of this chapter) alter the way many of your non-Christian friends and neighbors view Jesus?

Encounters

*"Look and you'll find what everyone from Moses to Martha discovered.
God in the middle of our storms." (p. 128)*

What are some steps you can take to be more mindful of God's love all during your day? What is one specific way you want to be different as a result of having worked through this chapter of the guidebook?

REMINDERS

- Jesus took the sins of the world upon himself; he paid for our rebellion against heaven.
- In his death for us, Jesus endured the unspeakable agony of abandonment by God.
- Because Jesus suffered the punishment we deserve, we need never experience rejection by God.

20
Christ's Coup de Grâce

God-Ordained Places

"Don't call Jesus a victim of circumstances. Call him an orchestrator of circumstances! He engineered the action of his enemies to fulfill prophecy. And he commandeered the tongues of his enemies to declare truth." (p. 148)

IMPRESSIONS

Chapter 20 deals with God's sovereignty (his awesome power and control over the universe). By focusing on the many ancient prophecies fulfilled during Christ's betrayal, arrest, trial, and crucifixion, Max demonstrates that Jesus wasn't some poor, hapless preacher. No, on the contrary, he was and is heaven's king who arranged the details of his own death, in order that he might provide us with eternal life. If you haven't done so yet, read the chapter. If you've already read it, skim back over the pages, jotting in the space below the events or claims or sentences that most grab your attention.

What was your favorite story or fairy tale as a child? How does that story end? Are you a person who likes (or maybe even needs) happy endings? Why do you think?

Have you ever thought of the entire history and future of the world as "God's story"? Is that a new thought to you—that God is the author of the real life cosmic drama in which we find ourselves? Or, to use theater jargon—God is the playwright, producer, director, and lead actor of the show currently playing on the universal stage. How do these metaphors shed light on history as we see it?

What events or situations in your life initially seemed terrible but ultimately turned out okay (or maybe even good)?

Before you begin this time of reflection, tell God all that is on your heart:
Any questions
Any concerns
Any fears
Any obstacles
Any failures and regrets
Any dreams

Then thank him for:
His perfect wisdom
His matchless compassion
His supreme peace
His infinite power
His endless forgiveness
His absolute goodness

GLIMPSES

Perhaps to the casual observer, the events surrounding Christ's passion seem random, even tragic. But notice carefully the way Jesus talked during his final days on earth:

"For I, the Son of Man, must die, as the Scriptures declared long ago. But how terrible it will be for my betrayer. Far better for him if he had never been born!" (Matthew 26:24 NLT)

"Tonight all of you will desert me," Jesus told them. "For the Scriptures say, 'God will strike the Shepherd, and the sheep of the flock will be scattered'" (Matthew 26:31 NLT).

"Don't you realize that I could ask my Father for thousands of angels to protect us, and he would send them instantly? But if I did, how would the Scriptures be fulfilled that describe what must happen now?" (Matthew 26:53–54, NLT)

Then Jesus said to the crowd, "Am I some dangerous criminal, that you have come armed with swords and clubs to arrest me? Why didn't you arrest me in the Temple? I was there teaching every day. But this is all happening to fulfill the words of the prophets as recorded in the Scriptures." At that point, all the disciples deserted him and fled. (Matthew 26:55–56 NLT)

Encounters

"*Matthew saw him in the waves. And you? Look closer. He's there.
Right in the middle of it all.*" (p. 128)

"The Scriptures declare, 'The one who shares my food has turned against me,' and this will soon come true" (John 13:18 NLT).

"During my time here, I have kept them safe. I guarded them so that not one was lost, except the one headed for destruction, as the Scriptures foretold" (John 17:12 NLT).

"The Scripture says, 'He was treated like a criminal,' and I tell you this scripture must have its full meaning. It was written about me, and it is happening now" (Luke 22:37 NCV).

Note the recurring phrase in all those passages: "the Scriptures" or "the Scripture." Why was Jesus so hung up on *the Scriptures*? And why should it matter to *us* that Christ's final days on earth corresponded exactly to the predictions of the Old Testament?

Hundreds of years before the birth of Christ, God spoke to and through the Jewish prophet Isaiah. Among other things he announced:

Surely He has borne our griefs And carried our sorrows; Yet we esteemed Him stricken, Smitten by God, and afflicted. But He was wounded for our transgressions, He was bruised for our iniquities; The chastisement for our peace was upon Him, And by His stripes we are healed. All we like sheep have gone astray; We have turned, every one, to his own way; And the LORD has laid on Him the iniquity of us all. He was oppressed and He was afflicted, Yet He opened not His mouth; He was led as a lamb to the slaughter, And as a sheep before its shearers is silent, So He opened not His mouth. He was taken from prison and from judgment, And who will declare His generation? For He was cut off from the land of the living; For the transgressions of My people He was stricken. And they made His grave with the wicked—But with the rich at His death, Because He had done no violence, Nor was any deceit in His mouth.

Yet it pleased the LORD to bruise Him; He has put Him to grief. When You make His soul an offering for sin, He shall see His seed, He shall prolong His days, And the pleasure of the LORD shall prosper in His hand. He shall see the labor of His soul, and be satisfied. By His knowledge My righteous Servant shall justify many, For He shall bear their iniquities. Therefore I will divide Him a portion with the great, And He shall divide the spoil with the strong, Because He poured out His soul unto death, And He was numbered with the transgressors, And He bore the sin of many, And made intercession for the transgressors. (Isaiah 53:4–12 NKJV)

In what specific ways does this passage point to the passion of Christ?

Encounters

"Make no mistake, Jesus saw himself as God." (p. 134)

We know that in everything God works for the good of those who love him (Romans 8:28 NCV).

Break down this beloved verse. Study it like an ace detective scouring a crime scene for evidence. Scrutinize each word and phrase. What does the verse say—really? What assurances are here? What stipulations?

> "Peace where there should be pain. Confidence in the midst of crisis. Hope defying despair. That's what that look says. It is a look that knows the answer to the question asked by every mortal: 'Does death have the last word?' I can see Jesus wink as he gives the answer. 'Not on your life.'"
>
> —SIX HOURS ONE FRIDAY

MUSINGS

"Thanks to the Pharisees for the sermon: 'He saved others; himself he cannot save' (Matthew 27:42 KJV). Could words be more dead-center? Jesus could not, at the same time, save others and save himself. So he saved others." (p. 148)

Why do you think some people continue to believe in psychics when these supposed seers are correct on only a small percentage of their predictions (and even then their prophecies are vague and general)? Why don't people sit up and take notice at Christ's fulfillment of Old Testament prophecy?

Scholars have noted that on the day of his death alone, Jesus fulfilled almost thirty different messianic prophecies from the Old Testament. This fact prompted Peter Stoner, a renowned mathematician, to grab his calculator and start punching buttons. His conclusion?

Get this—if we blanketed the entire state of Texas two feet deep in silver dollars and then put a mark on one of those coins, the chance that a blindfolded person could wander out among the 267,000 square miles of silver dollars and pick up, on the first attempt, the one marked dollar has the same odds that just eight of these biblical prophecies would ever be satisfied in the life of one person.

But some think, *couldn't it still be a coincidence?* In other words, maybe Jesus just memorized a few verses and remembered to quote them at just the right moments. Or perhaps if his followers

Encounters

"Accept him as God, or reject him as a megalomaniac.
There is no third alternative." (p. 134)

wanted so badly to believe in him, they dreamed up all this prophecy stuff, twisting the details to fit his life and situation?

How do you answer these questions?

Put yourself in John's sandals. It's Friday, late morning. You sit helplessly while your mentor and Messiah asphyxiates on a Roman cross. You burn with anger at the burly guards who hurl curses at your truest friend. Fact is, even though you have been with Jesus almost constantly for three years, he has been tortured and battered so sadistically that you scarcely recognize the limp figure hanging before your eyes.

Question: How do you feel late that night? How do you feel Saturday afternoon?

Finally, what are you feeling on Sunday night?

Let's say you have a friend whose life is one continual mess—sickness, marital heartache, financial woes, family baggage. Why, she could star all by herself in her very own soap opera! Yet she happens to be a Christian who really longs to believe the promise of Romans 8:28. She genuinely wants to trust in Jesus through her hard times, clinging to the notion that we serve a God who is able to turn a Crucifixion Friday into a Resurrection Sunday. But her struggles are like giant waves at the beach—one after another, each one knocking her off her feet.

What would you say to your friend? What wisdom can you offer?

DECISIONS

"Everything—the bad and the good, the evil and the decent—worked together for the coup de grâce of Christ. Should we be surprised? Didn't he promise this would happen? 'We know that in everything God works for the good of those who love him' (Romans 8:28 NCV).

Encounters

"His followers worshiped him, and he didn't tell them to stop." (p. 134)

"Everything? Everything. Chicken-hearted disciples. A two-timing Judas. A pierced side. Spineless Pharisees. A hardhearted high priest. In everything God worked. I dare you to find one element of the cross that he did not manage for good or recycle for symbolism. . . . Every dark detail was actually a golden moment in the cause of Christ. Can't he do the same for you? Can't he turn your Friday into a Sunday?" (p. 149)

What's the worst situation in your life just now? Is it difficult for you to see God's hand? Is it hard for you to hope? Put your truest feelings into words.

How does it comfort you to realize that God *is* in control of the affairs of the universe and the details of your life? How does it baffle and confuse you?

Think practically and specifically here. Looking over your life—the tough decisions you face, the trials you've got—what are two concrete steps of faith you can take today? (Remember that faith means you put your full weight on Jesus. You rely completely on him, so that if he doesn't come through, you're going down!) Is that a scary prospect to you? What's the worst thing that can happen if God's plans don't match up to your expectations?

Who is one person you can call to go to coffee or lunch with and discuss these matters?

REMINDERS

- God's greatest blessings often come disguised as disasters.
- Christ's brutal execution wasn't a human decision; it was pre-planned, pre-announced, and ultimately orchestrated by heaven.
- Our good and gracious God has already written the script for this world and for our lives.
- Knowing that God has ordained a happy ending for each of his children makes life not only bearable, but joyful.

21
Christ's Crazy Claim

Incredible Places

"The empty tomb never resists honest investigation. A lobotomy is not a prerequisite of discipleship. Following Christ demands faith, but not blind faith. 'Come and see,' the angel invites. Shall we?" (p. 154)

IMPRESSIONS

The final chapter of *Next Door Savior* takes a look at the resurrection of Jesus Christ. If you've been around church very much, this is a familiar story, an often talked about passage. You may be able to recite the facts in your sleep! All the more reason, then, to ponder deeply. We must not let familiarity breed contempt or even a ho-hum spirit.

Since the chapter is short, take a few moments to go back and re-read it. Refresh your memory. But before you begin flipping pages, stop, and bow your head and your heart before God. Why? Because enormous issues are at stake.

Ask the Lord to jar and jolt you, to wake you up, to give you a spiritual second wind. Request new eyes to see and a new excitement for the stunning reality of the empty tomb. Petition heaven for a deeper appreciation of how that one historical fact changes *everything*.

After your time of review and reflection, scribble your insights and questions and observations here.

What's the wildest announcement you've ever heard? The craziest, most outrageous news you've ever received? What did you do afterwards?

If you had a time machine and could travel back to witness any five biblical events, which would you choose to view live and in person (check any five)?

_____ The six days of Creation   _____ The Sermon on the Mount

_____ Adam and Eve's rebellion in Eden   _____ The feeding of the 5,000

_____ Noah and the Flood   _____ The Upper Room

_____ The parting of the Red Sea   _____ The first Easter weekend

_____ The giving of the Ten Commandments   _____ Christ's ascension into heaven

_____ David vs. Goliath   _____ The birth of the church at
                                                            Pentecost
_____ The birth of Christ

_____ Twelve-year old Jesus at the Temple   _____ One of Paul's missionary
                                                            journeys
_____ Other:

Why those choices?

GLIMPSES

Because it is the cornerstone of the Christian faith, the account of the empty tomb is found in each of the four Gospels. For our study here, we go to the final chapter of Matthew.

Matthew 28:1–10 (NCV)

The day after the Sabbath day was the first day of the week. At dawn on the first day, Mary Magdalene and another woman named Mary went to look at the tomb.

At that time there was a strong earthquake. An angel of the Lord came down from heaven, went to the tomb, and rolled the stone away from the entrance. Then he sat on the stone. He was shining as bright as lightning, and his clothes were white as snow. The soldiers guarding the tomb shook with fear because of the angel, and they became like dead men.

The angel said to the women, "Don't be afraid. I know that you are looking for Jesus, who has been crucified. He is not here. He has risen from the dead as he said he would. Come and see the place where his body was. And go quickly and tell his followers, 'Jesus has risen from the dead. He is going into Galilee ahead of you, and you will see him there.'" Then the angel said, "Now I have told you."

Encounters

"Keep your hand in his and your eyes on him, and when he speaks: 'Listen to him.'" (p. 135)

The women left the tomb quickly. They were afraid, but they were also very happy. They ran to tell Jesus' followers what had happened. Suddenly, Jesus met them and said, "Greetings." The women came up to him, took hold of his feet, and worshiped him. Then Jesus said to them, "Don't be afraid. Go and tell my followers to go on to Galilee, and they will see me there."

The first witnesses of the resurrected Christ were women. Why is this significant?

Consider two scenes, separated by just a few weeks:

• Luke 22:54–62. Describe Peter's behavior and demeanor in this instance.

• Acts 4:1–22. Describe Peter's behavior and demeanor in this instance.

How do you account for this dramatic reversal?

In a letter to the Corinthian church, the apostle Paul tried to clear up some misunderstandings about the resurrection. He explains this event's importance:

I passed on to you what was most important and what had also been passed on to me—that Christ died for our sins, just as the Scriptures said. He was buried, and he was raised from the dead on the third day, as the Scriptures said. He was seen by Peter and then by the twelve apostles. After that, he was seen by more than five hundred of his followers at one time, most of whom are still alive, though some have died by now. Then he was seen by James and later by all the apostles. Last of all, I saw him, too, long after the others, as though I had been born at the wrong time. For I am the least of all the apostles, and I am not worthy to be called an apostle after the way I persecuted the church of God. . . .

But tell me this—since we preach that Christ rose from the dead, why are some of you saying there will be no resurrection of the dead? For if there is no resurrection of the dead, then Christ has not been raised either. And if Christ was not raised, then all our preaching is useless, and your trust in God is useless. And we apostles would all be lying about God, for we have said that God raised Christ from the grave, but that can't be true if there is no resurrection of the dead. If there is no resurrection of the dead, then Christ has not been raised. And if Christ has not been raised, then your faith is useless, and you are still under condemnation for your sins. In that case, all who

Encounters

"Abandon. Such a haunting word." (p. 139)

have died believing in Christ have perished! And if we have hope in Christ only for this life, we are the most miserable people in the world.

But the fact is that Christ has been raised from the dead. He has become the first of a great harvest of those who will be raised to life again. (1 Corinthians 15:3–9, 12–20 NLT)

Why in verse 6 does Paul add the little phrase "most of whom are still alive"? What is the implication?

According to this passage, what are the dire consequences and grim implications if Christ didn't rise from the dead?

> "Is Jesus the son of God or the sum of our dreams? . . . No one could ever dream a person as incredible as Jesus is. The idea . . . that a virgin would be selected by God to bear himself, . . . the notion that God would don a scalp and toes and two eyes, . . . the thought that the King of the universe would sneeze and burp and get bit by mosquitoes . . . it's too incredible."
>
> —AND THE ANGELS WERE SILENT

MUSINGS

A few people are convinced Elvis is alive, or that the Apollo moon missions were fraudulent. Many are certain that homeschooling is the best way to educate children or that our consumption of sugar is killing us. What are some of *your* rock-solid convictions in life? Your deeply-held beliefs that cannot be shaken? (NOTE: Don't think only of the spiritual realm.)

The claims are outrageous—just plain hard to swallow. A certifiably dead Jesus comes walking out of his grave after three days? Since we don't have any personal experience with such a phenomenon, does your mind have a hard time grasping this? Is it tough for you to get a mental picture of this miracle of miracles? Does it seem too incredible to believe?

Encounters

_____

_____

_____

_____

_____

_____

_____

_____

_____

_____

_____

_____

_____

_____

_____

_____

_____

_____

_____

"Of course the sky is dark; people are killing the Light of the World." (p. 140)

"Remember the followers' fear at the crucifixion? They ran. Scared as cats in a dog pound. Peter cursed Christ at the fire. Emmaus-bound disciples bemoaned the death of Christ on the trail. After the crucifixion, 'the disciples were meeting behind locked doors because they were afraid of the Jewish leaders' (John 20:19 NLT)." (p. 155)

In just a few days, however, these men were transformed into totally different people. They became wild and bold beyond belief. They refused to stop talking about the risen Christ even when threatened with death.

In what way does this set of facts help substantiate the truth of the resurrection?

Perhaps the single transforming event in the lives of the disciples was their absolute certainty of the risen Christ. Convinced he was alive and sure of his Lordship, they didn't have to be prompted to share their faith. They were supercharged—unable to stop talking about Jesus. Spreading the news became their magnificent obsession.

Think about your life and your church. Do you sense the same enthusiasm? If not, why not?

DECISIONS

"These guys were so chicken we could call the Upper Room a henhouse. But fast-forward forty days. Bankrupt traitors have become a force of life-changing fury. Peter is preaching in the very precinct where Christ was arrested. Followers of Christ defy the enemies of Christ. Whip them and they'll worship. Lock them up and they'll launch a jailhouse ministry. As bold after the Resurrection as they were cowardly before it.

Explanation:

Greed? They made no money. Power? They gave all the credit to Christ. Popularity? Most were killed for their beliefs. Only one explanation remains—a resurrected Christ and his Holy Spirit. The courage of these men and women was forged in the fire of the empty tomb. The disciples did not dream up a resurrection. The Resurrection fired up the disciples. Have doubts about the empty tomb? Come and see the disciples." (p. 155)